Psychodynamics of Wr

Psychoanalysis is often referred to as a talking cure, but in this fascinating book it is the art of writing that is discussed and explored.

Including contributions from a selection of leading therapists, the book shines a psychoanalytic light on the very process through which the discipline is described. It includes chapters on the idea of creativity, the issues around a therapist's subjectivity, the challenges of describing trauma, as well as those of co-authorship.

Psychodynamics of Writing will appeal to clinicians, therapists and anyone interested in what the process of writing means.

Martin Weegmann is a clinical psychologist and group analyst, working in private practice and the NHS in London. He is a trainer and teacher. His latest book is *Permission to Narrate: Explorations in Group Analysis, Psychoanalysis, Culture* (Karnac, 2016).

Psychodynamics of Writing

Edited by Martin Weegmann

 Routledge
Taylor & Francis Group

LONDON AND NEW YORK

First published 2019
by Routledge
2 Park Square, Milton Park, Abingdon, Oxon OX14 4RN

and by Routledge
711 Third Avenue, New York, NY 10017

Routledge is an imprint of the Taylor & Francis Group, an informa business

British Library Cataloguing-in-Publication Data
A catalogue record for this book is available from the British Library

Library of Congress Cataloguing-in-Publication Data
A catalog record has been requested for this book

ISBN: 978-1-78220-504-3 (pbk)

Typeset in Times New Roman
by codeMantra

To Sylvia. With love.

To 'Anthony', an ex-patient, who with minimal education, few resources and no English (I worked with an interpreter) gave me insights into a world of personal and social trauma through drawings. 'Thank you' for showing me what your life is like.

Contents

About the editor and contributors

Editor

Martin Weegmann is a clinical psychologist and group analyst, working in private practice and the NHS in London. He is a trainer and teacher. His latest book is *Permission to Narrate: Explorations in Group Analysis, Psychoanalysis, Culture* (Karnac, 2016).

Contributors

Nick Barwick is a group analyst, teacher, and writer of both therapeutic work and fiction. As head of counselling at the Guildhall School of Music and Drama, he works with actors and musicians, and runs a private practice offering therapeutic consultations for writers experiencing writing blocks. Former editor of *Psychodynamic Practice*, his latest book, co-authored with Martin Weegmann, is *Group Therapy: A Group-Analytic Approach* (2017).

Stephen Frosh is Professor of psychosocial studies at Birkbeck, University of London, Fellow of the Academy of Social Sciences, and an Academic Associate of the British Psychoanalytic Society. His most recent books are *Hauntings: Psychoanalysis and Ghostly Transmissions* and *Simply Freud*.

Jeremy Holmes was consultant psychiatrist and psychotherapist at University College London and then in North Devon, UK. He is visiting professor at the University of Exeter, and lectures nationally and internationally. His many books include *John Bowlby and Attachment Theory* (2013), *The Therapeutic Imagination: Using Literature to Deepen Psychodynamic Understanding and Enhance Empathy* (2014), and *Attachment in Therapeutic Practice* (2017).

Phil Leask is a writer and researcher based at University College London. He writes on German history and literature, as well as on the meaning of humiliation. He is the author of several novels and short stories, and is writing a book on the everyday lives of a group of German women, derived from fifty years of letters.

Ian S. Miller is a psychoanalyst and writer living in Dublin, Ireland, where he practises. His recent books are: *On Minding and Being Minded* (Karnac, 2015), *Defining Psychoanalysis* (Karnac, 2016), and *On the Daily Work of Psychodynamic Psychotherapy* (co-written with Alistair D. Sweet; Routledge, 2018).

Cheryl Moskowitz is a poet and writer, and a leading contributor to the field of therapeutic writing. She co-founded LAPIDUS, the organisation for writing and well-being, she taught on the Creative Writing and Personal Development MA at Sussex University, and currently facilitates writing in a wide range of healthcare, community, and educational settings. Her publications include *Wyoming Trail* (Granta), *The Girl Is Smiling* (Circle Time Press), and *Can It Be About Me?* (Frances Lincoln Books).

Morris Nitsun is a consultant psychologist in group psychotherapy in Camden and Islington NHS Trust, a training group analyst, and a private psychotherapist at the Fitzrovia Group Analytic Practice. He was awarded the Royal College of Psychiatrists' president's medal for services to mental health in 2015. He is also a practising artist and exhibits regularly in London.

Joan Raphael-Leff is a psychoanalyst and trans-cultural psychologist specialising in reproductive issues. Previously professor of psychoanalysis at University College London and the University of Essex, she currently leads the Academic Faculty for Psychoanalytic Research at the Anna Freud Centre, London.

Joyce Slochower is Professor emerita at Hunter College and Graduate Center, City University of New York, faculty and supervisor at New York University, Steven Mitchell Center, Philadelphia Center for Relational Studies, and the Psychoanalytic Institute of Northern California in San Francisco. She is the author of *Holding and Psychoanalysis* (1996) and *Psychoanalytic Collisions* (2006). She is in private practice in New York City.

Laurence Spurling is senior lecturer in psychosocial studies at Birkbeck College, University of London, where he is director of trainings in psychodynamic counselling and psychotherapy, and is a psychoanalytic psychotherapist in private practice. He is the author of *An Introduction to Psychodynamic Counselling* (Palgrave, 3rd edition, 2017) and *The Psychoanalytic Craft* (Palgrave, 2015), and has edited several books and published papers on clinical practice.

Alistair D. Sweet is director of Meriden Psychotherapy and a psychotherapist in private practice in Belfast, Northern Ireland. He is an honorary lecturer in clinical psychology at Queen's University, Belfast, and, along with Ian S. Miller, the co-author of *On the Daily Work of Psychodynamic Psychotherapy* (Routledge, 2018).

Maggie Turp is a psychotherapist and psychologist. Her publications include journal papers and two books, *Psychosomatic Health: The Body and the Word* (Palgrave, 2001) and *Hidden Self-Harm: Narratives from Psychotherapy* (Jessica Kingsley, 2003). An area of current interest is the integration of narrative and psychodynamic approaches within psychotherapy.

Introduction

Martin Weegmann

In literate societies, we all have a relationship with writing, from self-defining "writers" at one end of a spectrum, through to those who hate the very thought of putting "pen to paper" at the other. Some people write almost every day, others are mightily relieved to leave any such activity behind as soon as they leave education, although even here there are many new forms of writing that engage people or that are unavoidable, such as texts, emails, posts, profiles, applications, and so forth. Lest the latter be seen as lesser forms of expression, many have compared the digital revolution to the invention of the printing press, in terms of its ongoing and unforeseeable implications. Personally, I am delighted that (often) younger people are creating whole new modes and genres of expression.

Of all the various dimensions of language—hearing, speaking, reading, writing—writing is the last to be acquired and, adding in publishing, is the most formalised form of communication. Psychologists have noted the "supporting role" that writing contributes to the learning process, in the form of scribbles, note-taking, skeleton plans, a role that is unique in so far as writing is much more than "talk recorded". Somehow it is its own form of thinking, offering back to the writer something they had not quite started with. And the surprises are many.

I have always loved ideas; they are the small sparks that can light a project. The spark for this particular project was listening to a talk by Jeremy Holmes on the use of the literary imagination in and for psychotherapy. Perhaps it was the ease of his delivery, or the very creativity of the interconnections, but I could have listened to him all weekend. I mused about the possibility of gathering a few papers for a "special issue" journal, but felt that more could be done. It was an idea in search of a wider vision, not to mention a group of willing authors. I contacted people, some of whom I knew personally, and the project began to take shape. My publishers, Karnac, provided the prompt feedback and, gladly, the enthusiasm that made it possible.

Where does the psychodynamic aspect come in? Although psychoanalysis began as the "talking cure", Freud's ideas and speculations were worked out in and through writing, as Mahoney (1989) has often argued. The large Freudian corpus includes case studies, theory papers, short studies, papers on technique, expositions and lectures, revisions, footnotes, and ambitious cultural forays; in Freud's ironic words, "I invented psychoanalysis because it had no literature" (cited in Roazen, 1969, p. 92). There is, however, a risk of creating myth out of brilliance, of which Freud's self-myths are examples. Bringing the genius down to earth, Sulloway (1992) draws attention to the social and rhetorical functions of Freud's writing—to secure adherents, persuade sceptics, and counter, even to "diagnose", detractors. Within this, we see the formation of an orthodoxy which, as we know from psychoanalytic history, has many unfortunate consequences. On the other hand, with Freud comes a new way of writing the self and whatever one's ultimate judgement of the merit of his achievement, at the very least, as Phillips (2006, p. 1) notes, he "changes our reading habits".

Freud was passionate about literature and mythology, which influenced his style and some of the founding concepts. Subsequently, there are countless examples of psychoanalysis turning its attention to literature; indeed, of much literary interest in psychoanalysis, although the degree to which psychoanalytic readings of literature lead to enrichment or reduction is open to debate. Literature aside, there is much less by way of reflection on the medium and practice of *writing* itself.

It is timely to bring together modern psychodynamic perspectives on writing by authors who are experienced writers. I do not think there can be a singular "psychodynamics of writing", any more than one could have a psychodynamics of walking, singing, or an interest in physics. Besides, reflections on writing are not going to share the same kinds of concerns and modes of relevance as those surrounding, say, a particular mental disorder or given clinical phenomenon. Two things prompted my concern with the subject of writing. One was curiosity about the struggle that trainee therapists often report in relation to the writing requirements of their courses. Why is writing so often felt as demanding and challenging? Do teachers of psychotherapy help enough, or do they somehow suppose that writing about the clinical is a natural act of transposition? How effective are our tutoring practices? Should personal journaling be encouraged, partly as an aide to writing? Second, I was curious about the sorts of psychotherapy writing that appeal to me and those that do not. I discovered no great reason, but guess that it is something to do with the presence of an engaging writing idiom, the (disciplined) use of the imagination, accessibility, and a degree of innovation to the work in question. So, maybe this book was in part my "request" to other authors to help me with these as well as other questions.

The authors include therapists, analysts, academics, and novelists, who offer their reflections on the broad theme of writing—its challenges, pleasures, anxieties, purposes, and our relationship, as authors and readers, to the written word.

Jeremy Holmes gets us off to a fine start, imaginatively comparing the processes of writing with psychodynamic therapy; the blank piece of paper that confronts the writer and the soon-to-be-used clinical session. He suggests that both writing and therapy can be conceived as "prostheses", as externalised, socially constructed structures whose purpose is to help us develop and to better "see" ourselves. Attachment theory is his framework and inspiration.

Joyce Slochower follows with her lucid chapter on finding the creative space which allows good clinical/psychoanalytic writing to proceed. Her ideas are relevant to scientific and fictional writing as well. In an illuminating use of Winnicott's notions of "being" and "doing", Joyce explores the self-states, psychological preparedness, and forms of anxiety that can inhibit or release writing potential. Her case studies are a model of clarity.

In Chapter Three, Stephen Frosh begins with Lacan, taking the reader through an intriguing exploration of how writing sends, receives, returns, and transforms itself; no straight lines, as it were. There are inevitable gaps and breaches between the author who writes and the document that is written. And neither writing nor psychoanalysis, he argues, occurs in suspended space, but only in places filled by the many details of social event and historical force.

My chapter considers authorship and the written word. What motivates writing and, in particular, the desire for publication? Amongst the possibilities I identify within myself is writing as an "act of intervention", in order to develop new connections, or to contest, even of the role of writing (righting) wrongs. One requires motivating passions—a reason to write—that need to be harnessed by a shaping of the written word so as to communicate most effectively.

Nick Barwick, in Chapter Five, offers an expressive excursion into writing anxiety, using a mixture of Kleinian, Freudian, and Winnicottian perspectives. Amongst the many issues he covers is the relationship between creativity and aggression, and those acts of "bringing together" which can be as frightening as they can be exhilarating. Of extra illumination is the fact that Nick brings in his own wide-ranging experiences as teacher, counsellor and psychotherapist, and author.

Lawrence Spurling's chapter proceeds to different territory and questions. What, he asks, is good clinical writing? And how is the clinical work of others, founders, teachers, and proponents, best presented, as part of learning the craft of psychotherapy? "Cases" can become written exemplars, as they were for Freud, but the question remains of *whose* narrative it is, and what the implications might be when intimate clinical experiences are translated by just one of the participants from the spoken to the written word? A wide range of thinkers, including Freud, Malan, and Ogden, informs his account.

As a joint chapter, Ian S. Miller and Alistair D. Sweet offer an engaging set of reflections on co-authorship. They offer a novel discussion of the notion of "pairing" from Bion, whilst elsewhere revealing personal details and characteristics that help us to better imagine their collaboration. Revealing too is their discussion of their "first date" as well as their use of the facility of email. One has a real sense of how "two" become productive company, with freedom to exchange, differ, and combine ideas; Alistair, a former professional musician, uses the analogy of "jamming".

Phil Leask is a researcher and writer, who, in his chapter, takes us into the heart of the archive. I say "heart of the archive" advisedly, as Phil leads us straight to the real lives and families of people living in former East Germany, considering the impact on himself of reading about their sufferings, humiliations, and adaptations; "the people I have come to know", as he puts it. As for the psychotherapist so too, in another way, for the researcher: how does one manage the complex feelings that arise in response to what one has come to know?

In Chapter Nine, poet and writer Cheryl Moskowitz takes us into the field of autobiographical writing. With the gentle assistance of thinkers like Bollas, Phillips, and a re-discovered gem by Dorothea Brande, she shows how inventive is the "I", as it weaves and edits its way through part-remembered, part-imaginative aspects of being. Reflecting upon her autobiographical novel, Cheryl describes the importance of negotiating the risk and fear of disclosure, whilst resisting the belief that there can ever be a complete, once-and-for-all account of oneself.

Joan Raphael-Leff's chapter considers "gestational" and generative anxiety faced by the writer, in all its depth. She uses the reproductive imagery of conception, gestation, and birth to observe the writing process, including the fear of looking inwards at one's work (akin to senography) as represented by the very act of writing the chapter. From her delightful first story as a little girl, through to her many publications, Joan's examination of the subject is a mine of interest.

In his chapter, Morris Nitsun treats us to a very honest account of his successive efforts to make his mark within the discipline of group analysis. He raises important questions: when is writing a contribution, a challenge, a criticism, or an act of rebellion? Morris describes the sometimes lonely and anxiety-filled consequences of questioning a founding "father" (S. H. Foulkes), alongside all its generational challenges. The wider point is that "conformity and innovation exist in dialectical tension, in which our institutions live on a knife-edge between compliance and creativity".

In the concluding chapter, Maggie Turp addresses inevitable gaps in psychotherapy between the written and the clinical. Given the importance of the "individual example" to that trade, how, she asks, does one decide between writing up composites, using fictive accounts, or seeking permission from clients? Each has drawbacks, with Maggie regarding the latter as preferable. It is fitting, then, that her chapter ends with a case study written in collaboration with her former client, "Declan", detailing his therapy and extraordinary childhood trauma. Declan has the last word of this book.

Chapter 1

On writing
Notes from an attachment-informed psychotherapist

Jeremy Holmes

Introduction

For the past forty years or so, I've spent an hour or two each morning at my desk writing—or trying to write—before the day-job gets underway. Apart from a few juvenilia, my efforts are professional/technical; sadly, I'll never be a novelist or poet. What drives this solitary, semi-solipsistic soul-search? Would life be different, diminished without this daily writing ritual? Is it defensive, or creative—or both? To what extent is writing a form of self-analysis, and are there overlaps between the rituals of regular psychoanalytic treatment, the "empty space" of the psychoanalytic session, and the writer's pages? In this chapter, I'll try to think—and write—about this from an attachment-informed perspective.

A first point is that writer and reader form a dyad; without writing, there could be no reading, and vice versa. Writing is communication: initially perhaps a conversation with oneself—a "duet for one"—but, random jottings aside, ultimately there needs to be a recipient for one's scribblings, imagined or actual. Somewhere at the back of my mind when writing there is always an audience; I try to "hear" the flow of my sentences from this postulated "other's" point of view.

Second, if writing is a form of conversation, it depends on the "digitisation" of sound, and possibly of thought itself. The evolutionary biologist Laland, emphasising the vital role of instruction and copying in all species, argues that the evolution of speech in humans depended on its being both a) a low-energy and b) highly accurate means of instruction and learning. Humans' success as a species depends on the flexibility and creativity conferred by our neuro-plastic brains allied to the capacity for rapid cultural transmission of new ideas via language, both spoken and later written (Laland, 2017). Our current digital revolution has its evolutionary origins in these two key features of language.

Accuracy means that speech had to be divisible into phonemes, words, and symbols; these in turn enable it to be written down. Thoughts become words, "out loud" or in the "inner ear"; words mutate into symbols on page or screen. In reading, they traverse similar pathways back into the reader's mind. Digitisation is what makes translation (literally, "carrying across") from one language to another to another possible; but also this journey from thoughts to inner speech to words on the page.

Thus writing itself is a species of translation. But, as Robert Frost famously asserted, poetry is what gets lost in translation. While the left brain handles digitised communication, the right brain takes care of the poetry—the tone, timbre, emotional valence, and musicality of words (McGilchrist, 2009). I shall return to this aspect later.

Contra McLuhan, mostly, the medium is *not* the message. Just as images on a computer screen can be the end-products of a variety of operating systems, so meanings can be transferred from one mind to another by speech, marks scratched on stone, papyrus, or paper, clattering Gutenberg press, or (as in this communication) electronically. My aim as a writer is for *transparency*: for meaning and music to shine through the medium, but for the reader to be largely unaware of the "operating system"—language, syntax, implicit poetics, and so on—used to transmit them.

Writing as prosthesis

Writing is generally considered to have emerged independently around 3000 BC in Mesopotamia; in Meso-America, Mexico, around 300 BC; and debatably in China around 1200 BC (Fischer, 2003). Writing can be thought of as a "prosthesis" (Freud, 1930a), comparable to other "extensions of ourselves" (McLuhan, 1964), such as fire (digestion and temperature regulation), action-at-a-distance weaponry (predation and protection), and agriculture (foraging).

Writing is prosthetic in a number of ways. Its first and most basic function is as an adjunct to memory. Who has not had the memory-jolt associated with finding a long-forgotten love-letter, abandoned poem, shopping list, school essay, or even published paper ("did I really write *that?*")? Second, writing enables communication at a distance—writing makes shouting obsolete. Third, beyond word as bond, writing is an indispensable black-and-white triangulation or "third" (Ogden, 1989), able to record and hold participants to mutually agreed transactions.

Writing is prosthetic in more subtle ways too. The overtone of my title, "notes", suggests parallels between written and musical text. The latter was "invented" around AD 1000 (Goodall, 2001). Once notation was introduced, it permitted musical complexity—harmony, counterpoint, modulation—not possible when relying on memory alone. Writing is a "technology" that enables the sophisticated manipulation—comparisons, juxtapositions, deletions, additions, contradictions, confirmations, and so on—of the inner world of thought, comparable to mechanical manipulation and transformation of the external environment. Speech is inherently improvisatory, while writing enables more complex thoughts to be articulated, albeit with a reduction in the liveliness of dialogue.

Written-down music is especially helpful to the average musician—I speak from envious experience—illustrating the democratising, anti-elitist impact of literacy. Comparably, writing helps one to think for oneself. Luther's translation of the Bible into the vernacular went hand in hand with his challenge to priestly power and his championing of unmediated encounter with the deity.

Page and couch

Sitting at my desk, writing enables me to see, test, concretise, and develop the truth—factual and emotional—of what I am thinking and feeling. Writing is word made flesh. But most would-be writers are familiar with how just how *difficult* writing can be. Anything rather than having to sit down at one's desk and confront that blank piece of paper or screen: sharpening pencils, checking emails, desk-tidying, making just *one* more cup of coffee. If writing, at least in the first instance, is communication with oneself, then the process is far from easy or straightforward. Does what I'm trying to say make sense? Has it all been said before? Will my feeble attempts be judged and found wanting?

These fears are not unlike those evoked by lying on an analyst's couch at the start of a session, especially for a novitiate. Do I dare disturb the universe of fifty minutes' empty space with my jumbled, shameful, incoherent ramblings, motivated by disruptive desires and terrors? It is therapists' job to counteract this anxiety and its accompanying attachment dynamic. In their secure base role, they communicate, often without words, *bounded receptiveness*. The message is that this is a safe, non-judgemental space, a place where you can begin to listen to yourself thinking aloud, to learn about and from your inner world.

Attachment-informed psychotherapy (Holmes & Slade, 2017) assumes that most potential psychotherapy clients are burdened by prior adaptations to suboptimal caregiving environments. Love and attention has been conditional, intermittent, or non-existent. Feelings, especially if painful or negative, will have been suppressed or unregulated. Experience cannot be thought about or mentalised; creativity is inhibited.

In the attachment model, the inner self is structured on the basis of primary relational experiences. If accurate and compassionate affect co-regulation has been the rule, the subject is likely to be able to *be* a subjective self: to experience, tolerate, name and process and own feelings, however painful or scary, and to give them voice.

Mentalising (Holmes, 2010) entails the capacity to stand back from one's thoughts, to view them objectively, and see them for what they are—"just thoughts"—and to view others' thoughts and actions in the same way. Reflexivity is intrinsic to mentalising, itself prosthetic, helping to navigate the complexities of one's own and others' minds and interactions. Being mentalised by a caregiver is a necessary precondition for self-mentalising.

Mother–infant communication is initially physiological and gestural (Feldman, 2015), a multimodal "dance" mediated by touch, sight, sound, and smell, based on biobehavioural synchrony (Feldman, 2015). Gradually, however, language begins to take over as the primary means of communication. In the context of emerging secure attachment, the therapist represents a hitherto missing *interlocutor in the inner world.* Mears (2005) notes that children aged three to five have an externalised inner conversation as they play "alone in the presence of the mother". Therapeutic "dialogue" too can be thought of as an externalised inner conversation, that is, inner monologue hitherto excluded or avoided.

When affect expression has been punished or discouraged, or felt to be chaotically overwhelming, the subjective self is correspondingly diminished and constricted. There will be a shying away from experiencing and naming feelings, a tendency to project them outwards, or experience them as emanating from a repudiated "alien" part of the self.

Page and couch—in different ways—help transcend these paralyses, both symbolising a relationship with the *primal, hand-holding, mentalising, security-providing (m)other* needed for the inner world to come fully into being. In psychotherapy, this self-in-relation-to-self is a central theme. Language, whether written down or therapeutically uttered, reveals the *self's relationship to itself.* The therapist veers between being a "real" secure base figure, and a transferential representation of the suboptimal caregiver. The therapist represents the part of the self that knows itself better than it consciously is aware, just as mothers "know" their children before they have developed the language to articulate their feelings.

Let's illustrate this with an example from Wagner's opera-drama the Ring Cycle.

In *Die Valkyrie*, Wotan, ruler of the Gods, is confronted by his jealous wife Fricka's rage at his profligate infidelity. She is particularly affronted at his having fathered a child, Sigmunde, by Erda, the Earth Goddess.

Sigmunde has fallen in love with a married woman, Sieglinde, wife of Hunding, the hunter. Fricka insists that Wotan ensure that Sigmunde dies in the ensuing husband–lover fight, as the law of the Gods requires. Depressed, bound by his "superego" (an external constraint of conditional security, Fricka's message that she will love him only if he does her bidding, typical of insecure attachments), Wotan reluctantly agrees to his wife's demand. Wotan is forced to choose between his child and his wife (the "wicked step-mother"—a prevalent theme in folk literature and family therapy).

But now Brunhilde, another of Wotan's illegitimate children, and leader of the female warriors, the Valkyrie, appears at Wotan's side. Brunhilde sees that her father is deeply unhappy and in his heart of hearts wants to save his son Sigmunde. Assuming the role of secure base, she asks:

"Father, father, tell me, what is troubling you? How your worries upset your child! Confide in me, I am loyal to you."

He now confesses—in terms instantly transposable to psychotherapy—that she has indeed seen into his inner feelings:

"I only talk to myself when I talk to you."

Obedient to Fricka, Wotan destroys Sigmunde's power, allowing Hunding to kill him. But, with Brunhilde's help, Wotan has also listened to the dictates of his heart, and so saves the life of pregnant Sieglinde. The child, Seigfried, Wotan's grandson, is destined to become the saga's future hero, and repair—at a spiritual level, at least—the flawed despot's crumbling world.

"I only talk to myself when I talk to you" could be a motto for the inner world-space of psychotherapy. In his moment of crisis, Brunhilde *knows her guilt-driven father better than he knows himself*, as does the caregiver of a securely attached infant, and at times, therapists their patients. So too the "listening page" for the writer, where one "hears" one's thoughts objectified, modulated, regulated, and available for further exploration and reflection. Once one's conversation with oneself begins, the marks on the paper, the voices of one's character, speak back, triggering an exploratory dialogue in which, like the free-associative process enabled by the analyst's "absenting presence" (Barratt, 2013) in the consulting room, "anything" can happen.

Wagner's "outcome" is far from a happy-ever-after fairy story; rather, a tragic compromise where difficult feelings are acknowledged, a balance between desire and reality is struck, but where pain can be managed and life goes on. Fricka is satisfied—Sigmunde must die; but so too is Wotan—Seigfried lives to fight another day. Compromise is the writer's lot too. Rarely, if ever, is one fully satisfied with what one has written. Good-enoughness, rough approximation, are worthwhile writing goals. The wastepaper basket—real or virtual—should never be uncritically empty, nor overflowing in a fruitless search for perfection.

Psychotherapy and the Romantic tradition

Freud's foundation myth was the father–son struggle. Klein shifted the focus to mothers and infants. Lacan, by contrast, emphasised the role of grandparents, reminding us that identity is shaped long before birth, emerging from our parents' own upbringing, genetic inheritance, and cultural background. However much he saw himself as a conquistador, psychoanalysis' "onlie begetter" Freud also had his intellectual grandparents, rooted as he was in the German Romantic tradition of Kant, Schelling, Schiller, Novalis, and Goethe (Watson, 2010). The pre-1914, pre-metapsychology Freud of the *Interpretation of Dreams* and "free association" (Barratt, 2013) was under the sway of this Romantic impulse. Jung, still at this stage Freud's chosen heir, similarly saw an aim of psychoanalysis as fostering patients' "active imagination"—whether through daydreaming, painting, writing, or other artistic activities.

German Romantic ideas were translated into the Anglophone world—linguistically and geographically—by Coleridge (R. Holmes, 1999), a comparatively rare example of someone outstanding both as artist and theorist. Here is his famous account of the workings of the imagination:

> Most of my readers will have observed a small water-insect on the surface of rivulets, which throws a cinque-spotted shadow fringed with prismatic colours on the sunny bottom of the brook; and will have noticed, how the little animal wins its way up against the stream, by alternate pulses of active and passive motion, now resisting the current, and now yielding to it in order to gather strength and a momentary fulcrum for a further propulsion.
>
> This is no unapt emblem of the mind's self-experience in the act of thinking. There are evidently two powers at work, which relatively to each other are active and passive; and this is not possible without an intermediate faculty, which is at once both active and passive. In philosophical language, we must denominate this intermediate faculty... the IMAGINATION.
>
> (Coleridge, 1817, p. 203)

This balance between spontaneity and control, activity and passivity, applies equally to the act of writing, and to the role of the therapist in the consulting room. In both, one is passively "listening to oneself" and, at the same time, actively "listening to oneself listening", guiding, analysing, and selecting from the listening process.

A number of British or British-influenced psychoanalysts, with varying degrees of acknowledgement, have drawn on Coleridge's legacy, including Sharpe (1940), Bion (1962), Winnicott (1974), and Rycroft (1979); more recently, Britton (2003), Ogden (1997), Turner (2004), Ferro (2012), and Waddell (1998). A key lineage runs backwards from Bion's injunction to the analyst to be "beyond memory and desire", through Keats' "negative capability"—the ability to remain in doubts, mysteries, and uncertainties—to Coleridge's "willing suspension of disbelief".

Bion picks up on the Coleridgean concept of poetic "reverie" and uses this to describe the analyst's state of unprejudiced receptiveness, reborn in Ogden's (1997) "dreaming the session". The animating notion is that of the capacity of the analyst, like the poet, to allow thoughts and feelings spontaneously to arise; to transform these imaginative stirrings into gesture and words which can be put to therapeutic use; and thereby help patients better understand *their* unconscious thoughts and feelings. Poetry and therapy both represent a "raid on the inarticulate" (Eliot, 1954).

Some artists worry that psychotherapy might stifle or analyse away their creative spark. Perhaps it's safer to "not know" about the workings of the unconscious mind, but let it get on with its creative job unimpeded by too much conceptual thinking. Anecdotal and some systematic (Carson & Becker, 2003) evidence tends to argue against this: Rachmaninov, Samuel Beckett, and more recently Wendy Cope are examples of outstanding artists whose work was rescued and enhanced by psychotherapy. There are, however, some cases where the mental pain associated with trauma is, like the Medusa's head, best viewed obliquely. Dance, art, and music therapy suit some patients—especially those burdened by severe mental illness—better than verbal therapies.

Whether in the consulting or the writing room, the workings of the imagination can be subdivided into a number of components, all of which feed into, and flow from, Coleridgean reverie (Holmes, 2014). A precondition is *primary attachment*. This term captures the undivided attention of the analyst as the patient enters the room and readies herself for a therapeutic conversation. Similarly, as one sits down at one's desk[1] a flow is established between mind, hand, and page reminiscent of a primary attachment relationship, for which mother and infant remain the prototype.

In states of reverie, images, thoughts, memories, identifications, internal role-play, inner voices, roads not taken, and verbal music swim to the surface of consciousness. Freud—who enjoyed his trips into the Austrian countryside—likened free association to the moving images seen from a railway carriage window. Reverie is a species of day-time dreaming. Free association is dreaming out loud—"alone" in the presence of the analyst. Writing too entails "dream-space" in which one allows thoughts and images to surface, randomly, without let or hindrance, circumventing censorship and ratiocination. (My personal writing and self-analysing reverie spaces include the time between sleeping and waking; going for a daily run; and musing while bathing.)

Coleridgean again, next comes *logos*. Thoughts and images, if they are to be put to literary or therapeutic use, will finally be committed to paper, given voice. The very act of writing or speaking is dialectically linked with reverie; thoughts and their articulation piggy-back and mutually reinforce one another to produce a story, a line of verse, or a feeling-imbued therapeutic thought. This is the boot-strapping nature of language as a prosthesis, a specific illustration of how our species creates the very niches—contested depending on existing power-relations—to which it strives to become adapted.

At this stage in the creative/therapeutic process, superego-ish perfectionism has to be cast aside: "don't get it right, get it written". *Action, commitment*—finger on keyboard, words on a page—is needed if the world, however minuscule the difference, is to be changed. Comparably, therapists must trust their counter-transference and find ways, however fumblingly, to speak out loud what their unconscious is telling them about their patients' inner worlds (Holmes & Slade, 2017).

That will be balanced, later, by the final and essential piece of the imaginative jigsaw: *reflection*. For writers, revising, cutting, re-shaping, re-phrasing—and not infrequently jettisoning and starting afresh—are vital skills. A trusted friend, colleague, or family member to whom first drafts can be exposed is invaluable. I have been rescued more than once by the precepts of "when in doubt, cut it out", and "always drop your first paragraph", or, pace Blake, "murder your infants in their cradle". Stephan Zweig in his autobiography (1943) attributed his position as Europe's most successful writer of the 1920s to the fact that the final versions of his novels represented only about ten per cent of their first drafts. Equally, the self-reflective process is an essential part of psychotherapeutic work for both patient and therapist, in which, collaboratively, they think about their mutual interactions and become increasingly adept at "mentalising the transference".

James Joyce on writing

James Joyce was familiar with the German Romantic tradition through Coleridge (Laman, 2004). Continuing with therapy/writing parallels, consider his classification, put in the mouth of the protagonist in his only play, *Exiles* (Joyce, 1918), written while he was also working on *Ulysses*. Rather than Schelling's triad, "the good, the true, and the beautiful", his comprised the *lyrical*, the *epic*, and the *dramatic*.

> The *lyrical* form is in fact the simplest verbal vesture of an instant of emotion. The simplest *epical* form is seen emerging out of lyrical literature when the artist prolongs and broods upon himself as the centre of an epical event and this form progresses till the centre of emotional gravity is equidistant from the artist himself and from others. The narrative is no longer purely personal. ... The *dramatic* form is reached when the vitality which has flowed and eddied round each person fills every person with such vital force that he or she

assumes a proper and intangible esthetic life. The personality of the artist, at first a cry or a cadence or a mood and then a fluid and lambent narrative, finally refines itself out of existence, impersonalizes itself, so to speak.

(Joyce, 1918, p. 67, my italics)

Joyce's terminology implicitly equates his typology with different literary genres: lyrical with poetry, the epic with the novel, and the dramatic with theatre, although these may merge and emerge one with and from another. *Ulysses*, with its multiple voices, contains examples of all three: Molly's famous concluding monologue is pure subjective poesis; the early funeral section and later Bloom–Stephen perigrinations are interpersonal and epical; while the night-time episode is cast as drama. Finally, the detached, quasi-scientific penultimate section becomes a parody of the impersonalisation he advocates, including this rather disturbing account in which man-bumps-head-on-beam:

The right temporal lobe of the hollow sphere of his cranium came into contact with a solid timber angle where, an infinitesimal but sensible fraction of a second later, a painful sensation was located in consequence of the antecedent sensations transmitted and registered.

(1922/1960, p. 828)

From a psychotherapeutic perspective, Joyce's sequence can be seen in terms of psychological maturation, moving from naked self-expression, through seeing oneself in relation to others, to a non-narcissistic perspective in which the world exists independently of oneself. All three coexist, often in a layered way, both in psychotherapeutic conversations and in works of art.

Compare this with a clinical vignette:

Bryan's gate

Bryan, a farmer, comes 10 minutes late for his session. He apologises, saying that someone had forgotten to shut the gate into a field, and as a result his horse escaped into the lane; he couldn't leave for his session until the adventurous equine had been corralled back into its rightful place.

All this is very straightforward and clear—and a seemingly good reason for being late. And yet… there was something else. In the previous session, he had uncharacteristically abandoned his habitual stiff-upper-lip and cried copiously when describing a painful bereavement.

Was the horse-story, the therapist mused aloud, perhaps also the patient's way of referring back to the dangers of "*opening emotional flood-gates*", and his wish once more to bottle up his feelings, to be "left alone" with them in the "missing" ten minutes of the session?

Bryan's tears were nothing if not lyrical. But then came the epical story: his shame at revealing his "cry-baby" weakness to another man. Then, the "dramatic" a) a societal context: a man whose mother had died when he was only ten years old, handed over by his father to efficient but un-feeling aunts, and b) his biological heritage, the wish to kick over the traces and escape from emotional constriction into rage and grief.

Running through all three is the thread of language, simultaneously extending and restricting the scope of expression. As in every therapeutic conversation, there are two stories here: one, in Langer's (1951) terms, "discursive", factual, sequential, everyday; the other, "non-discursive": affect-related, tangential, symbolic, "left-field"—and also given to puns—a horse that had left its field!

The unconscious—in Lacan's elusive phrase "structured like a lan-guage"—is perhaps an example of Russell's paradox (1959), a "set of all sets that does not include itself". Language is always more extensive and wiser than its practitioners and perpetrators. The task of the writer is to inhabit and harness that greater force in order to find emotional truths. Similarly, therapist and patient together work to try to capture in words the elusive wider meanings arising out of their relationship.

Conclusion

Let's go back, in more a personal way, to the question with which I started. Why, why, why do I write? To be slightly facetious, if mathemati-cians are people who turn coffee into equations, and echoing Malcolm's insistence to the child and wife-bereaved Macduff that he resist the "grief that does not speak", psychotherapists are people who *turn pain into words*.

Looking back, I would say that writing has, over the years, kept me sane, and protected me from depression. This is in part "defen-sive": writing about mental pain, especially if located in others—"the patient"—somehow keeps my own feelings of failure and helplessness at bay. Writing is a magic trick that makes pain disappear—but not just into thin air. There is ablation, splitting, denial, avoidance of necessary action—but also, once suffering, loss, and grief are admitted, transcend-ence and transmutation. To return to *The Tempest*'s oft-trod lines:

> Those are pearls that were his eyes.
> Nothing of him that doth fade,
> But doth suffer a sea-change
> Into something rich and strange.

Here is the irony inherent in our chosen work—it has also enabled me to face myself; provided a language for thinking about my inner world; enabled me to become more objective and contextual about life, including my place in it; paradoxically, given the lonely nature of the activity, put me in touch with other people—readers and fellow-writers; and finally, provided the satisfaction that comes from having *made* something, however rickety.

There are lyrical, epic, and dramatic reasons why writers, and my fellow literary-minded therapists, might spend up to ten per cent of our adult lives sitting, often unproductively and unhealthily (not to mention unwealthily), at our desks.

In part, writing is a lyrical "gesture of instant emotion" and cry for recognition and attention; a way of asserting one's existence, of saying "Hey, I am here!". As this transforms into the epic project, one begins to see oneself in relation to the intimate others who make up one's inner world or secure base. For writers, these are the "characters" and their voices who populate their novels and plays, many of whom are imaginatively transformed versions of attachments to parents, siblings, friends, lovers, spouses, children. For us therapists, this list extends to patients. Therapy requires patients temporarily to be admitted into one's inner world, while reciprocally the therapist inhabits the client's inner world, with which the therapist—again temporarily—imaginatively identifies.

In dramatic mode, this process is subjected to objective scrutiny: the artwork takes on a life of its own, independent of the author; in the case of great writers long outliving them. Mentalising in therapy can similarly be seen as a species of dramatic objectivity in which therapists subject themselves, their feelings and beliefs, to scrutiny. This happens through "self-supervision", whether in thought or process recording and with real-world supervisors. Mentalising entails both engagement with, *and* detachment from, the material reality of clients and their difficulties—and oneself. As a therapist, one needs to identify and value what one has to offer, while at the same time recognising one's inevitable limitations and blind spots. In the Joycean sense, this entails a "dramatic"—and "dreamatic"—movement from attachment to non-attachment. Writing, as mentalising's prosthesis, helps with this objectification, pointing to the unending task of living with—and striving to transcend—transience, failure, and finality.

Note

1 Now that the health dangers of a sedentary life have been established (Buckley, Hedge, Yates, et al., 2015), some writers have turned their desks into combined walking machines and laptops. Wordsworth, a great walker/writer, would have approved.

Chapter 2

Finding a creative writing space

Joyce Slochower

Karen opened our supervisory session by asking me if I thought she was developed enough as a psychoanalyst to try her hand at writing. Her work with a very difficult patient had stimulated ideas that she wanted to express, and she thought her perspective might be a new and interesting one; I agreed, and we began discussing her ideas in depth. Karen left the session feeling hopeful, planning to begin writing that very weekend. When she came in the following week, however, Karen was utterly deflated. On her own, facing the blank computer screen, she had become intensely anxious and unable to proceed. With utter certainty, Karen realised that her voice was inarticulate, "old hat", insufficiently incisive. Karen felt humiliated by the naiveté that had led her to think of writing. She had a chilling image of the amusement, derision, even wrath of certain senior analysts as they read her paper. How dare she tread where senior psychoanalysts dwelled? Even before beginning, Karen gave up.

Karen knew these anxieties well; she had dealt with them in therapy over many years. But despite considerable insight, Karen hadn't found a way to put her terrors aside and enter the arena of creative activity. The prospect of articulating her own voice raised the alarming spectre of the other. Creative desire collided with creative anxiety and resulted in inner collapse.

We take a leap of faith when we embark on a writing project. That leap, which coalesces differently as a function of who we are and the context (personal and professional) in which we write, inevitably involves subjective (and sometimes objective) risk.

When we write, we explicitly address our colleagues, thereby locating ourselves in the complex world of psychoanalytic thought. The aspiring psychoanalytic writer faces a daunting wealth of literature articulated from multiple theoretical and clinical perspectives. To construct or modify theory, to offer a new way of viewing clinical material, to integrate or criticise the work of others, all require that we take account of the work of others while also making an original contribution.

Writing: personal and interpersonal dimensions

Like all forms of creative activity, psychoanalytic writing is both a solitary act and a form of communication to the other. It serves a variety of functions for the individual writer. In the process of articulating our ideas, we may discover a new way to support (or alter) our treatment stance and deepen our understanding of our patient and ourselves. Many of us write about areas of personal concern; in so doing, we may find an opportunity to work on our own issues or communicate indirectly with our own analysts. In writing, we explicitly locate ourselves *vis-à-vis* other theoretical positions.

The "anxiety of influence" (Bloom, 1973) speaks to the common concern that we haven't been as original as we hoped. That anxiety sometimes exerts silent pressure on us to diminish that influence. We "creatively invent" or misread the work of others in order to bolster the uniqueness of our contribution. Will we be (mis)understood, re-created, made over? How exposed will we be? How much of us can we bear to make known?

Personal writing in a professional context

The contemporary psychoanalytic world is extraordinarily complex and diverse; we confront a wide range of theoretical models that pull us in confusingly different directions and may make it difficult to find and/or hold an internally steady position.

Psychoanalytic writers typically write for other professionals whose vocation involves deconstructing and exploring the complications of individual and interpersonal dynamics. There's a consequent risk that we'll feel personally as well as professionally stung by critique. It's not necessarily paranoid to anxiously anticipate how both our text and our dynamics will be scrutinised and misconstrued.

The anxieties associated with psychoanalytic writing will, of course, be intensified or diminished as a function of the writer's vulnerability to criticism and judgement (on one hand) and her capacity to enjoy intellectual engagement and challenge (on the other). Does the writer remain a child or sibling in relation to her readers, or can she create a separate space within which to articulate her own professional idiom (Bollas, 1987)? For some, the uncertainty associated with writing evokes excitement, a sense of adventure, anticipation of a warm reception or even a good fight.

Writers like Karen, however, become immobilised by the anticipation of failure or critique by the other, real or imagined.

Carol, a creative and prolific writer, described the impact of the imagined reader on her writing process: when she becomes stalled, she reads the literature, which helps stimulate ideas and clarifies her own thought process. Carol reads freely and without anxiety. Yet, when imagining the paper she plans to write, Carol quickly becomes terrified by the idea of the other, by the danger of retaliation by her colleagues, from whom she anticipates an annihilating response. Carol manages these anxieties by writing in total privacy, altogether avoiding the relational world until convinced that her work is perfectly sculpted and beyond reproach. Carol deals with the threat of a collision between the creative gesture and the other's demolishment by withdrawing from the relational arena. While her withdrawal helps her write, it also limits her ability to actively take on critique and engage with it.

When she was a child, Carol's parents reacted to symbolic acts of assertion by attempting to subdue, retaliate, or demolish her voice (both verbally and physically). Carol associates her writing anxieties with her parents' repeated rebuff of her "spontaneous gesture" (Winnicott, 1960). Her internal audience threatens to replicate that experience, raising the stakes associated with the creative act.

Other writers' anxieties are organised differently. While some fear the rejecting, punitive, or dismissive response of authority figures (e.g., journal reviewers, senior institute faculty, their analyst, etc.), others fear retaliation by competitive siblings (colleagues or other professional competitors).

Ron harboured long-standing resentments toward some of his colleagues and mentors. When he wrote, Ron was consumed with a need to show his colleagues up; when he came across a paper that seemed better than his, he fell into a state of despair, abandoned his efforts, and retreated (literally) to his bed.

With encouragement from his analyst and friends, Ron eventually began writing again. However, his need to argue with the other, to prove that he was right and they wrong, tended to flatten his work and render it one-dimensional. Ron couldn't stay with or play with his own ideas in a non-adversarial way.

Writers like Ron who chronically experience the outside world as dangerous find all creative endeavour to be fraught with risk. For others, the sense of threat is more specific, linked to the actual subject of the essay.

Amir had immigrated to the United States from the Middle East and wrote his PhD thesis on the psychological experience of immigration. Although he had previously written on more emotionally neutral topics without excessive struggle, Amir selected this particular essay topic in a quasi-conscious attempt to confront and rework his own immigration experience.

As the essay evolved, however, Amir became overwhelmed with anxiety and was unable to complete it. In an unconscious fantasy that he eventually contacted, Amir stepped over his father's grave as he submitted the essay for publication. His father (who was still alive) had failed to learn English or in other ways acculturate. The subject matter of Amir's essay stimulated a level of intense conflict around separation and oedipal issues that had not been previously evoked. Those issues effectively stopped Amir in his creative tracks.

Writing and gender

Although men and women alike are vulnerable to the kinds of relational dangers I've described, feminist writers have suggested that some qualitatively different problems exist for female writers as a function of gender and, more specifically, maternal identification. Since the act of writing literally takes the mother from her child's side, creative expression collides with the mother's wish to meet the child's needs. How can the mother take on the reality of other separate perspectives, much less write about them, if she expects herself to focus only on the child?

In shifting away from her own wishes, the mother's capacity to put her separate ideas into words may become blocked, foreclosing the transitional space crucial to creative expression. Writing represents an abandonment of the relational world, an experience of danger and aloneness, and it becomes impossible to tolerate the isolation and uncertainty of the writing process; creative and relational desire collide. Thus, the germ of an idea may be toyed with, perhaps presented in a session or meeting, but quickly dissolves or loses power.

Other writers are less vulnerable to anxieties about abandoning the other than to the immobilising impact of self-doubt. Like my supervisee Karen, Susi was so tormented by the fear that her ideas were insubstantial that she began and then abandoned essay after essay. Susi couldn't enter the realm of the imaginary, couldn't entertain creative fantasy, because she found it impossible to access and articulate ideas within the private space of her mind. Susi seemed to lack the experience of "going on being", or subjective omnipotence (Winnicott, 1962). She couldn't confidently access a reliably responsive internal audience in the face of doubts about the value of her ideas.

These kinds of anxieties probably have more often plagued women than men. And, certainly, a baby represents an especially palpable interference for the writer/mother. Nevertheless, I would reframe this dilemma in broader terms, for I don't believe it to be inherently gender-related. The woman writer's experience is a particularly poignant metaphor for the struggle of some female *and* male writers to contact internal process. The "male" and "female" represent alternating (and culture-bound) strains in all of us.

Collisions in the creative moment: "being" and "doing"

Psychoanalytic and feminist perspectives on writing suggest two distinct sources of creative activity that organise around concerns about the self and about the other. These themes parallel Winnicott's (1971) discussion of "being" and "doing", two core dimensions of subjective process. Winnicott contrasted the containing "being" function with "doing", that is, with the active creation of a bridge to the world and thus implicitly to separateness. Although Winnicott didn't uniquely ascribe "being" to women and "doing" to men, he did connect the female/maternal element with the former and the male/paternal element with the latter.[1] He viewed these elements as evidence of universally normal bisexuality, the "split-off other sex part of the personality" (p. 77). In another context, I linked Winnicott's notions of "being" and "doing" to two different analytic functions while explicitly separating these functions from actual gender (Slochower, 1996 a, b; 2014 a, b). "Doing" describes the analyst's very active interpretive, relational, or boundary-setting functions, whereas "being" represents the analyst's capacity to contain parts of subjective process in order to establish space for self-elaboration. Within the "being" metaphor, the analyst meets—but doesn't actively alter—herself in response to her patient's demands. I understand the act of responsive containment to describe neither passivity nor submission to the other, but a highly active, sometimes conflicted internal struggle in the face of relational pull.[2] Psychoanalytic process involves both "being" and "doing" on the (male or female) analyst's part, although individual analysts may identify more with one dimension than the other.

The "being" and "doing" self-states may provide a window through which an anxious or conflicted writer can access creative process because these idealised self-states create a shield against debilitating self-doubt; they establish a buffered space within which to think and write, to take the leap of faith involved in creating. Within this protected space, core subjective threats to the writing process are excluded, supporting the writer's use of creative illusion. Creative illusions fortify the analyst during moments of clinical uncertainty and can be similarly crucial to the capacity for creative expression.

Writing and the idealisation of power

"Doing" anxieties are organised around the consequences of action. A writer who is plagued by these relational concerns fears the (real or internal) reader's critical eye and the danger that the other will reject or annihilate her work.

One response to "doing" anxieties is the evocation of antidotal fantasies that expand the power that the writer occupies in relation to the threatening reader. The unconscious use of "doing" fantasies counters the vulnerability evoked by creative action.

While struggling to write his first paper, Peter spent many sessions describing his fear that his supervisor would rip his idea to shreds. In an attempt to address that anxiety, Peter carefully read a newly published paper written by his supervisor. In our next session, Peter excitedly described the serious theoretical flaws he had discovered in his mentor's work. Elated by this "evidence" of his supervisor's less than perfect wisdom and buoyed by the fantasy that he had surpassed this mentor/father, Peter returned home and virtually dashed off his own paper. Peter's response to enormous unconscious anxieties was to diminish the perceived power of the other as he defensively embraced a grandiose intellectual position.

At times, the experience of creative impotence has erotic connotations. The writer's ideas are neither "big enough" nor "exciting enough", and she engages fantasies that reverse that fear. My supervisee Nina imagines that colleagues will respond to her paper with enormous excitement, that she will be both admired and (erotically) desired. Her antidotal fantasies allow her to write because, within them, the erotised relational threat is subjectively turned on its head: her colleagues won't dismiss her; she will impress and excite them.

Writers who embrace illusions based on "doing" manage narcissistic issues not by suppressing them, but by actively taking on the other. The writer's primary identification is as actor; that is, as a subject residing in a world of other objects and subjects. "Doing" anxieties are countered by "doing" fantasies. The writer imagines surpassing those who came before; she envisions destroying or remaking the psychoanalytic world. These "doing" fantasies reverse the danger that the writer might fail to be "big enough" or "complete enough".

Within the "doing" illusion, the writer defends against relational challenge by implicitly or explicitly establishing a place in relation to her colleagues. Aron (1995) suggests that psychoanalytic writers must allow themselves to create a fantasy of recasting or even destroying the work of their analytic forefathers. Omnipotent fantasies establish a powerful, active self-state. They help the writer hold contrasting ideas in mind without addressing and resolving them in ways that limit her own position. A transitional space is thereby established within which ideas may develop without requiring that the writer make sense of them in ways that would prematurely truncate the creative process.

Omnipotent "doing" fantasies represent an unconscious response to anxieties about action. As compensatory fantasies, they're empowering. On a more unconscious level, though, they leave underlying vulnerabilities reversed rather than engaged. They obscure, without resolving, the writer's self-experience as an anxious child in relation to her professional parent(s).

Writing and the expanded interior space

"Doing" anxieties and "doing" fantasies are lodged in the relational domain. They're far less relevant to the writer who doesn't fear the other's response to her work because she's struggling simply to remain "in her own skin", to trust the potential value of her words. Writers like Karen find it problematic to access and sustain their words at all, and so never quite arrive at the point where relational anxieties might be evoked. If illusions are to foster the writing process, these writers must counter self-doubt by establishing an antidotal "being" self-state that bolsters access to an internal voice.

It's paradoxical that an idealised "being" self-state can facilitate creative process. "Being" is most often associated with containment and the inhibition of self-expression. The mother facilitates the baby's capacity for object-relating because she contains her own clashing needs and doesn't require that the infant sort out the projected from the real aspects of her personhood. The writer's identification with the maternal ("being") state tends to create an internal pressure *not* to delineate the edges of a separate voice and thus inhibits creative engagement.

Karen was working on a qualifying paper at her institute when she became obsessed with the fantasy that an emergency was unfolding at home while she sat at the computer; she didn't feel this anxiety while seeing patients. Her anxious phone calls home provided only momentary relief; after many false starts, Karen abandoned her computer altogether.

We eventually came to understand that Karen's anxiety was linked to an unconscious conviction that her withdrawal from the world while writing would injure her child. Karen imagined her little girl to be mournfully alone and bereft while Karen immersed herself in the rich world of ideas. Interestingly, that anxiety wasn't stimulated when Karen remained in the (object-related) caretaker position *vis-à-vis* her patients.

"Being" anxieties, then, tend to result in an overwhelming inhibition of creativity. The writer's experience of inner insufficiency shuts down the capacity to think and, therefore, to write. Core fears organise around abandonment of the other or the discovery that one's inner life is empty and lacking creative potential.

Betty, a professional non-psychoanalytic writer, finds it extremely difficult to contact, much less to believe in, the value of her ideas. The blank computer screen both represents and stimulates a feeling of internal blankness, and she can spend days in a frozen and overwhelmed state. When Betty succeeds in getting something down on the page, she feels some relief; the words are "something to come home to"; they relieve the conviction that her interior is altogether blank because only her parents really "know" anything.

Betty is easily frozen by self-doubt. Yet, over time, she has found an alternative avenue into creative process by accessing a different kind of "being" self-state in which containment temporarily protects her from threats to self-integrity. Betty withdraws from the world and immerses herself in the power of her own mind, in a sense of conviction about her ideas. This imaginary "being" experience establishes an insulated space and provides her with a crucial layer of protection against paralysing, hypercritical self-scrutiny. The illusion of creative perfection protects Betty by erecting an arena of certainty about her creative capacity and enhancing the reality and legitimacy of her existence.

We need to re-examine the dynamics associated with the "being" metaphor. Despite the potentially inhibiting effects of this self-state, "being" opens up an alternative creative avenue for writers paralysed by self-doubt. An idealised "being" self-state can support the experience of interiority by bolstering the power of inner process while temporarily excluding the threatening object world from the writing process. Vulnerable writers who access this experience may more easily maintain their interiority during the act of writing by establishing another version of the maternal illusion that protects the mother from inevitable moments of failure.

Finding creative self-states: a personal example

The developmental origins of a sense of integrity, or "being", and volition, or "doing", probably lie in childhood. The parent who is responsive to the child's spontaneous gesture promotes that child's capacity to maintain a sense of internal intactness independent of the other's response. Mixed experience can be tolerated; the value of one's personhood isn't constantly on the line. In a similar way, anxieties related to action ("doing") may be mitigated when parents recognise and accept the child's acts of assertion without retaliating. A more reliable feeling of agency and access to interior process leaves the child less vulnerable in the creative moment.

The need for relational support doesn't end in childhood; we continue to seek recognition throughout our lives, perhaps particularly when we make a creative gesture. For the psychoanalytic writer, the professional other (real or imagined) can provide crucial (if symbolic) support. Some writers conjure a receptive reader, while others exclude a critical one and turn inward in a private act of recognition. Probably all writers periodically make use of real relational support in facilitating access to creative process.

During the first few years of my writing career, I was involved in academic social and clinical psychology, where I wrote papers and a data-based book with comfort and ease. The format of my work was highly prescribed, its content tightly linked to research design and subsequent data analysis. Very little of me was expressed or exposed in my writing and the contents didn't carry symbolic meaning (other than as a means for gaining tenure).

As my interest in empirical research waned and I became interested in psychoanalysis, everything changed. I left structure behind and could no longer rely on "hard" evidence to support my ideas. My writing felt personal and put me on the line in a very different way; I was suddenly overwhelmed by a fear of exposure. Self-doubt collided with creative desire: Would I create a valuable or a worthless piece? Would my inadequacies be exposed? Would I inadvertently reveal something about myself that I was unaware of?

My anxieties, then, were lodged primarily in the "being" arena; I didn't write at all until I had aired my concerns to a particularly responsive and encouraging supervisor. He unequivocally confirmed the value of my ideas and offered to help me get them into publishable form.[3] His offer had a profound effect that was almost entirely symbolic. Although I never asked for the concrete help he offered, his encouraging certainty about the value of my contribution allowed me to begin to write.

However, I didn't write in interaction with him or anyone else. Instead, I retreated from the relational arena and established a transitional space characterised by a borrowed illusion of certainty about the value of my work. That contained space temporarily sealed off self-doubt and helped create the feeling of fully "being in my own skin", able to feel out the edges of my thoughts. As I wrote my first psychoanalytic paper, I altogether bracketed the uncertainty, danger, and anxiety associated with the risk of failing in the creative act. When those anxieties resurfaced with particular force, I returned to my supervisor to recapture the more insulated "being" self-state, although I seldom engaged in active theoretical dialogue with him. In this sense, I paradoxically used a relational experience to support a *retreat* from the more complex, risky, and very non-ideal relational world.

In the "being" self-state, I felt powerfully identified, even merged, with my supervisor/father. I embraced *myself* with his words, and on a more unconscious level, evoked the experience of being my father's adored child.

The illusion of creative certainty represents a retreat from relational challenge. It provides a temporary solution to personal issues that reside more in the domain of the legitimacy of subjective process than interpersonal action. Yet while the "being" illusion excludes the world of threatening objects, there is, perhaps, an implicit (pre-oedipal) parental identification behind this self-state. As I withdrew into myself, I was far from alone; I found a way to internalise my supervisor's sense of serene confidence in my creative potential by evoking that experience as I wrote.

Validated by some professional successes, I gradually grew more confident of my ability to access and articulate my ideas. Yet, most paradoxically, as anxieties lodged in the arena of being subsided, I became acutely aware of my place within the professional community. No longer feeling like a child among psychoanalytic adults, I found it more difficult to exclude the threatening other when I wrote. Now I encountered another set of anxieties organised around their responses to my work. These were "doing" anxieties; they reflected a worry about the other, more sibling than parent, but not always less of a threat. At times, these voices were intellectually stimulating, provoking an internal dialogue that pushed my thinking forward. At other moments, though, I felt daunted by the wealth of other creative, productive analytic writers. I was aware of the danger of their potential critique and became stalled, unable to continue articulating my ideas.

To protect myself from these relational anxieties, I sometimes engaged a "doing" fantasy: I took on the relational world but in illusory form: I fantasised the admiring responses of my colleagues to my work, the stir it would create. Although this fantasy was more explicitly relational than the "being" illusion, it was no less idealised. It absolutely excluded the likelihood that my papers would be less well received than I hoped or that they would raise questions and criticisms as well as praise.

Over time, I've come to feel less need to retreat to either of these self-states. I'm able to tolerate the relational threats inherent in the writing process and take on psychoanalytic criticism in the creative moment. Because creative space feels more genuinely transitional, I can more easily tolerate paradox, anxiety, and conflict within it and can enjoy the destruction and reworking of text that are an inevitable part of the writing process. It has become easier to move in and out of protected space and to read my own work critically without becoming frozen in self-doubt. By asking my colleagues for critical feedback as well as reassurance, I re-enter the relational arena—literally and symbolically turn to other readers for an "objective" (although inevitably subjective) response. My identification here shifted away from idealisation based in fantasy and illusion toward active relational engagement.

But this doesn't mean that I never experience self-doubt. Writing-related anxieties haven't altogether disappeared; there are contexts in which I can worry about the value of my work and its reception in the professional world. I'm not altogether sorry about that, though. It seems to me that these creative anxieties, while less than pleasant, push me to work longer and harder, to require more of myself than I would in the absence of doubt.

"Being" and "doing" in creative space

For some (like me), when the basic issue of "being"—that is, of personal legitimacy in the professional world—resolves (what I have to say *is* of value), concerns shift to the "doing" arena (how will my work be received?). But for many writers, "being" *and* "doing" anxieties represent alternating (rather than alternative) ways of organising experience. And, of course, each concern can represent a defence against the other. The writer may focus on fears about colleagues' retaliation in order to sidestep more basic worries about her capacity to think and write, or alternatively, may deny competitive concerns by emphasising her personal vulnerability.

Some writers describe how, when seized by an idea, they must quickly get it down on paper before self-doubt intrudes. For them, the illusion of certainty isn't sustained over time and can be accessed only briefly. Still other potential writers find it impossible to begin at all because they can't bracket uncertainty even temporarily. Immobilising self-doubt is incompatible with the act of creative expression and results in an abandonment of the writing project.

Creative illusions and creative rigidity

Despite the facilitating potential of creative illusions, considerable risks are inherent in their use; a prolonged retreat to a single-minded illusion of certainty leaves the writer absolutely wedded to her ideas, unable to consider alternative viewpoints. Vulnerability to critique makes the world of ideas threatening and narrows or freezes creative process.

For Dennis, both "being" and the "doing" self-states are integral to his writing process. When he can write in isolation from other points of view, he does so freely and with pleasure. But he can neither read other perspectives nor critically reflect on his ideas. The recent discovery that someone else had articulated an idea similar to his own catapulted Dennis into a state of despair. He quickly deferred to the wiser words of his senior colleagues and suspended work on his project. Only when he physically retreated to a location where he had no books was he able to free himself from the pressure of multiple voices.

Dennis established an entrée into the creative process through a "being" self-state. However, because he's unable to shift out of that state and allow discordant ideas to penetrate, his work tends to be articulated in a defensive, rigid voice that's bleached of his own rich intellectual capacities. Dennis can't tolerate theoretical collisions. When confronted with critical responses by journal reviewers, for example, he becomes overwhelmed and despairing; he can't use these critiques to deepen or complicate his paper. Dennis' need to maintain an insulated state ultimately impoverishes rather than enriches his writing process and the finished product.

Ultimately, we must be able to address the place of our work within the larger world of psychoanalytic ideas and an excessive use of "being" or "doing" illusions may well interfere with this capacity. Only when creative illusions are loosely held can they support the paradoxical capacity to experience, at alternating moments, self-doubt and the momentary conviction of certainty that are central to a creative and responsive writing process.

Notes

1 See Bollas (1996) for a related discussion of these different analytic functions.
2 Benjamin (1995) has also criticised Winnicott's association of "being" with the female element and of "doing" with the male element.
3 I am deeply indebted to Larry Epstein for his warm encouragement and support.

Chapter 3

A letter always reaches its destination

Stephen Frosh

The letter

There is a large literature on writing, and a smaller one on psychanalysis and writing. Unfortunately, I have not read much of it, so I will start from somewhere else, with some associations to Jacques Lacan's comment during his analysis of Edgar Allen Poe's *The Purloined Letter*: "the sender, as I tell you, receives from the receiver his own message in an inverted form. This is why what the 'purloined letter,' nay, the 'letter *en souffrance*,' means is that a letter always arrives at its destination" (Lacan, 1966, p. 30). This is one of only a small number of academic "references" that I will give in this paper, as I want to explore something else about the dynamics of writing, but it is a useful one. What is it that always returns to the sender, and what is it that constitutes a letter's "destination"? The most interesting rendering of this is from Slavoj Žižek (1992), who parses Lacan's claim in various ways depending on which perspective is taken in relation to the different orders of the Lacanian scheme, the Imaginary, Symbolic, or Real. From the Imaginary point of view, the letter always arrives at its destination because wherever it arrives is *defined* as its destination. That is, "*whosoever* finds himself at this place is the addressee since the addressee is not defined by his positive qualities but by the very contingent fact of finding himself at that place" (p. 11). More formally, we recognise ourselves as the one to whom the letter is addressed, but this does not mean that it really was specifically addressed to us; it just means we believe (imagine) that to be the case.

> When I recognize myself as the addressee of the call of the ideological big Other (Nation, Democracy, Party, God, and so forth), when this call "arrives at its destination" in me, I automatically misrecognize that it is this very act of recognition which *makes me* what I have recognized myself as—I don't recognize myself in it because I am its addressee, I become its addressee the moment I recognize myself

in it. *This* is the reason why a letter always reaches its addressee: because one becomes its addressee when one is reached.

(p. 12)

In this mode, as the letter circulates, it creates its subjects, its addressees: we imagine ourselves to be the ones for whom the letter has been written. Something seems to speak to us in what is written and "hails" us, to use the old Althusserian term; in responding to this, we act as if we are really the one for whom the letter's message was intended. In fact, however, there is a misrecognition going on. The letter had no such specific intended addressee, it was just sent out—a message in a bottle—and happened to land somewhere, with the receptive reader being struck by it and feeling hailed, spoken to, referenced; this is a fantasy, though a significant one.

Žižek has a number of different Symbolic readings of "a letter always arrives at its destination" which need not detain us here, save to note that one of them is "the letter arrives at its destination when the subject is finally forced to assume the true consequences of his activity"—his "moans and groans" as Žižek parodies them (p. 13). This suggests that in sending out the letter, the subject is caught out, not realising what is revealed by it, at least to the psychoanalytic eye. We write the letter and send it; either it goes to the wrong people (we hit "reply all" unthinkingly) or it reveals more than we intend (a parapraxis intervenes, and we say "love" for "live", etc.). It then comes back to us to reveal the "true", repressed intention: hostility or desire. It also references a further Symbolic rendering of the formula "a letter always...": "one can never escape one's fate... the symbolic debt has to be repaid" (p. 16). The theme of fate calling is very present here (the opening of Beethoven's Fifth Symphony is often experienced this way, fate knocking at our door, yet this is in truth nonsense), and certainly resonates with the "letter" formula itself. Something that cannot be escaped always comes back to haunt us, however much we might think we have evaded it, however unaware we are of its existence in the first place. Did I know of this desire or this hostility? It is there face to face with me when fate calls, when the whole world reads my email; it instructs me as to whom I might be. This links, finally to the Real element:

A common pre-theoretical sensitivity enables us to detect the ominous undertone that sticks to the proposition "a letter always arrives at its destination": the only letter that nobody can evade, that sooner or later reaches us, i.e. the letter which has each of us as its infallible addressee, is death. We can say that we live only in so far as a certain letter (the letter containing our death warrant) still wanders around, looking for us.

(Žižek, 1992, p. 21)

If this has shades of Woody Allen's dancing grim reaper in *Love and Death*, it is perhaps no accident: Žižek is particularly well attuned to the way popular culture is often close to the truth. Žižek complicates this by pointing out how the letter is not just death as a negative, but also *enjoyment*—but we can perhaps leave him here, as my point is simpler. When we write and then send a "letter", the only thing we can be confident about is that it will always find its way back to us, in one manner or another, disturbing the scene with its effects. (This is, by the way, encouraging as well as threatening: as hardly anyone actually reads academic writing, it is good to know, as an author, that it will at least have one real, surprised reader—oneself.)

Writing without direction

If the act of writing produces a letter that then finds its way in the world, creating its readers but also folding back on the writer, what is it that produces the writing itself? Much of the time academic writing is defensive, taking refuge in obscure terminology or supposedly "objective" distance, erasing the writer as if the resulting text can be a kind of absolute, offering a set of truths unadulterated by the writer's passions. There is no need to deal in detail with the lacunae in this version of things—it is a truism of psychoanalysis and psychosocial studies that locating oneself outside the "line of the Symbolic" in this way is impossible. We are always implicated in what we write about. A more challenging question is whether we *only* write about ourselves; that is, if the writing concerns something of personal significance, how much of the "person" can and should go into it? And what could this "personal" investment be, given the difficulties (psychoanalytic, post-structural, etc.) of locating any such thing? For my students, this is always a problem. Should they write about themselves self-consciously, knowing that they can only portray a part of what is relevant, knowing that every revelation is also a disguise, a twisting of the truth into something that is readable? Even the most self-reflective person has a subjecthood that is shrouded and opaque, and academic writing is not necessarily the place where one can strip this bare, even though the appeal of my "discipline" of psychosocial studies for some students seems to be precisely that it licenses the expression of emotion and self-revelation. Self-revelation is necessary but by definition inevitably unsuccessful: it puts us into the writing, but it is neither the writing itself nor, thankfully, "us". And sometimes, it has to be admitted, it is no more than "confessional", and embarrassing, and dull.

So the bigger issue is how to be involved in what we might be writing whilst also respectful of the distance between the authorial subject and what is written, and between what we might believe we are saying and what the message could be. It relates to the powerful intervention into psychoanalysis that comes from Jean Laplanche (1999), specifically his notion of the "external" locus of subjecthood, which he understands as having to do with the enigmatic message placed in the human infant by the sexual unconscious of the other. For example, it is not known to the mother how much her erotic life is pressed into action by her contact with the child, but this is nevertheless passed on by her to her infant as an unconscious message, an indigestible piece of psychic activity. Unintentionally, unbidden, the adult implants in the infant a disturbance that cannot be fully interpreted, but that remains encrypted as the kernel of the unconscious. If we take this as a model, then the broader idea—about living, about writing—is that whatever we think we are doing, something else operates within us (routinely for psychoanalysis, the unconscious), and this something else comes initially from "outside". It is "enigmatic" because we are stirred and aroused by it, but never can manage or control it, or fully interpret it. Under some circumstances, however, we may be able to give voice to it, and this could be those points where Lacanians see the Real. That is, whilst we can never move out of the circuit of the Symbolic when reflecting upon ourselves, so conscious self-referencing works only to a certain extent, releasing ourselves to the process of writing might at times let something else speak with the voice of a certain kind of non-Symbolic truth. All I am suggesting here, through this rather rarefied vocabulary, is that we might not always know what we are doing when writing, and this is likely to be a good thing.

My own writing often surprises me. This can be very disappointing, when I read back something I wrote long ago and think, "Did I write this?" "How come I can't write anything as good as this anymore?" Even worse: "How come I am still writing exactly the same thing, sometimes in almost the same words, and it is still not right, yet twenty years have gone by?" Mostly, I sit down to write with very little optimism, get distracted by emails which I pretend are unwelcome, watch Youtube videos, and look for chocolate, and in between force a few words out, desperately monitoring the word length counter. The text grows, and as long as I resist the temptation to lift and re-use large chunks of previously written material, or to start from the beginning again, I can close my mind to what I am producing, hoping for the best. My intentions are always good: I will radically revise what I have written in this ridiculous unmediated way, I will craft and correct and make sure *this time* that I have produced something of value. On a bad day, everything gets put off for a week or two. On a good day, it turns out that, apart from the vast array of typos that need correcting (not caused, on the whole, by unconscious impulses but simply by clumsy fingers), what I have written is more or less what I am stuck with. The odd thing is, I rarely recognise it as my own even though I was there during the writing; I cannot work out how it got from me onto the screen; and I realise that I have somehow felt more real during this process of production than I do most of the rest of the time. This is what is so surprising: how something comes from somewhere "else", unintended and relatively unprocessed, yet also comes from "within", carrying with it some affective power even when the content is abstract or academic. All this is to say that the act of writing can be a way of escaping from the constraints that come from acute self-monitoring; and that this is akin to a psychoanalytic process, with all the difficulties of letting go and facing our internal difficulties that psychoanalysis and writing share.

Writing in this unplanned, directionless way is a mode of trusting oneself. The problem is, are we, am I, trustworthy? If we know as little about ourselves as psychoanalysis posits, then it is likely that amongst the various surprises that such writing can produce might be a set of unpleasant discoveries. There is a long list of possibilities here: superficiality, envy, hostility, narcissism, silliness, incoherence, wishfulness... Occasionally—the hope that keeps me going—we might discover unexpected creativity and even enjoyment, but given the nature of things, this does not happen all that regularly. Instead, the letter that returns when I read back what I have written is too often something painful enough to require censoring. This is not necessarily because of what it explicitly states, but is more likely to be a problem of tone. In the gaps of meaning, something is revealed which is not all that desirable, which might be a useful piece of private knowledge, but perhaps best not shared. So much of this is like the psychoanalytic experience that it worries me: is psychoanalysis a mode of writing? Does it involve reading back to the subject the message that she or he has sent out unawares, a horrible dark mirror that unsparingly reveals the violence that lies in what might seem to be the most anodyne politeness, the lustfulness that is present in care, the puffing up in modesty? If this is the case, many of us might be forgiven for writing at all, and perhaps this is one source of writer's block: the danger of exposure, the fear that we will be seen through in the moment of being read.

What is it like...?

I am not too keen on giving an example here from my work, as it is precisely the problem of self-revelation and self-scrutiny, and the limits of self-knowledge, that I am exploring. But I will nevertheless reflect a little on the difficulty of writing in such a way that the letter that returns is fuller than the intention might have been. Recently, I wrote a paper on Steve Reich's string-quartet and tape composition *Different Trains* (Frosh, 2017). This piece of music, which is perhaps classifiable as a "Holocaust memorial" composition, moves me greatly and also raises a number of issues about the limits of witnessing that have both academic and personal moment for me. I explored this in the paper and am reasonably happy with the result. But reading it over, I am struck by a simple question that was asked of me by someone who read it early on, and that I have not been able to answer: what was it like for me to hear *Different Trains* for the first time, and what was it that made this relatively small piece of music stand out from the great mass of Holocaust art, music, and literature so that I felt I wanted to write about it? Which is to say not that this question cannot be answered, or at least cannot be answered in a reasonable, approximate kind of way (because for all the reasons mentioned earlier, I am not likely ever to know for sure and in detail exactly what it was that made me want to respond in writing to this piece rather than any other), but rather to note that, however engaged my writing was, it did not explain or communicate this more personal element. Instead, the writing revealed a gap, which at least for someone curious and sympathetic constructed the question: "Yes, but, what is it like...?"

So, "What is it like?" What is it that becomes embodied in a writing that comes to life, able to express and maybe trigger a set of ideas that are honest in relation to the emotional origins of investment in the material? My *Different Trains* paper clearly begs this question even as it addresses it, by which I mean that it conveys a message about how difficult it is to find a way to approach such emotive memorialisations without either sentimentality or denial. I think this is all right; I am not too hard on myself, but I wonder how it would be to reflect more openly on the question and to write about it in an academic piece of this kind. This is probably not the place for a full-blown answer, even if I were capable of providing it, though my sense is that part of the story is that I had a specific and powerful reaction to the music and especially to the way Reich uses the sampled speech rhythms of various speakers, including Holocaust survivors, to drive the melodic lines played by the string quartet. The resulting hauntingness of this is profound: even when the words being spoken are hard to hear, their "resonance" spreads like a stain across the music and stays alive and echoing right through to the end. My response to this was to offer an emotional welcome to the soundscape of the music, to feel liberated from a simply cognitive understanding and instead absorbed into something edgy. To me, the music seems just about to steer successfully between abstraction and self-aggrandisement, between voyeurism and identification with suffering. My guess is that Reich manages this very difficult task well, even if there are moments when the project collapses and even if his achievement is very precarious and open to challenge. Something about the way he uses his own experience (the first part of the piece draws on his memories of childhood journeys on trains across America, going between his separated parents) and sets it up against the Holocaust testimonies (his "different trains") is dangerous and serious, and makes me hold my breath to discover if it would work. I do not even know for sure that it does work, only that it is worth the effort.

This is still, obviously, not a proper answer to the "What's it like?" question. My written article leans on the power of the musical composition by describing and evoking it, so some of the energy in it is not my own. But I guess it arises from a specific passion—for finding a way to identify without colonising, to be both at a distance (the music is formal, constructed) and present (it is also emotional and lyrical and uses potent narratives); and without consciously working this out, I tried to reproduce this in my own written piece. In that sense, what I did was derivative of the music, yet there is enough in it that implicates me to raise the original question, "So what was it like?" What it was like, in fact, was overwhelming, emotional, troubling, confusing, and exciting; but this list does not really help at all.

There and back again

Here, finally, is a story that I offer as a meditation on writing, a kind of parable or "modern midrash". As I do not want to reproduce any of my "academic" writing here, it comes instead from the written version of a set of panel comments I made at the Birkbeck Critical Theory Summer School in July 2016, drawing on some lectures I gave that week and on a book review of a study of one of Freud's grandsons, Ernst. The context was a discussion of the death drive, which for whatever morbid reasons kept cropping up in my debates with the students. Here, I am trying to think about what made the "discovery" of the death drive so poignant.

It is worth remembering the historical circumstance, the massive destruction of the First World War and the appalling demonstration that the drive to build up civilisation might not be the centre of human longing. There is also the small, exact biographical moment of the *fort–da* game, Freud's observation of his grandson Ernst's play, which indeed became the best-known moment of Ernst's life. It took place when he was just eighteen months old, in September 1915, and still called Ernst Wolfgang Halberstadt (he changed his name to Freud later in life). *Grosspapa* Sigmund visited his daughter Sophie in her home in Hamburg and watched his little grandson at play. Ernst's simple game has become the most famous one in the history of psychoanalysis, and was forced to bear an enormous weight of meaning in *Beyond the Pleasure Principle*—the book that introduced the death drive, the incitement that repeats inside each of us to return to the dust whence we came but also to make mischief and sew destruction along the way. By the time the book appeared in 1920, millions had been killed across Europe in the Great War; and Sophie too, Freud's "Sunday child", was dead of the Spanish flu, along with twenty million other people. Little Ernst's contribution towards this, in the happier time when his sweet and attentive mother was still alive, was to take a wooden reel and throw it into his curtained cot, so it would disappear from sight. "O-o-o-o", he would say, which his mother and grandfather translated as "fort", "gone"; and then, with a "joyful 'da'", he would draw the reel out again into the light. The game would be repeated tirelessly: *fort* and *da*, or at least that is what we assume Ernst was saying—gone and back again. Psychoanalysis would never be the same after this observation was written up, its essential nature as a practice of repetition becoming increasingly recognisable: over and over the same process, throwing something out of sight, drawing it back in again. Now we see it, now we don't; an infantile game that can sum up a whole lifetime.

Why bring this up here? In the background were the great social events of the First World War, the terrible barbarism that, unimaginably, was in the end a precursor of even worse to come. Also in the background, but explicitly referenced by Freud, was the *fort–da* game and his grandson, shadowed by history and by a future of emotional difficulty after both his mother and his younger brother Heinerle died. Freud's writing of *Beyond the Pleasure Principle* (1920g) was a "scientific" exercise, but it was fuelled by these social and personal events, and it shows the effects of this in its ideas (death drive) and in some of the manner of its writing (the *fort–da* game). My response to this has always been quite intense, relating to the war and its effects, but in the passage above I was under the influence of reading Benveniste's book on Ernst, and the deep suffering that came to him from his mother's loss and his grandfather's inconsolability over her death and that of Heinerle, her second son. Writing later to Ludwig Binswanger, whose own young child had just died, Freud commented, "For me, that child took the place of all my children and other grandchildren, and since then, since Heinerle's death, I have no longer cared for my grandchildren, but find no enjoyment in life either" (Benveniste, 2015, p. 79). So poor Ernst, all those losses and rejected too as bringing no consolation to his grandfather. Is any of this in my own written response to Benveniste's book? I think it's an overwrought passage, not particularly careful or as austere as I might want it to be; the losses that Ernst and his grandfather experienced were too strongly conveyed, too alive even nearly a century later, to be kept at bay. I wonder if what happened is that there was a kind of unconscious communication from one text to another that results in a mode of affective engagement almost despite my writer's urge towards caution. Writing is a process of thought and craft; but if you let it run, without so much meditation and direction, it can come out oddly, not as expected, but still true to something, unwieldy perhaps and in need of careful management, but nevertheless real. Freud's extraordinary ability to observe and then draw far-reaching conclusions that would have an impact right through the culture is one thing that marks him out as a great writer. Living in the echoes of this, in its ripples, my own writing could only soak up his style and his feeling and half reproduce it, half engender it with something new. I am sorry for Freud, sorry for Ernst, but never knew quite how much, until there it was on the page in front of me.

Like Lacan's "letter" formula, the *fort–da* game prefigures the repetition compulsion: everything comes back, everything returns to the one who originated it. In my case, what is revealed is at least my sense of the suffering of this small boy and the shadow it throws over the future of psychoanalysis; and how Freud's own melancholy meant that he could offer little sustenance at that time to his most needy family member, and how attuned he was to the darkness that would soon engulf Europe. Freud's writing sublimates his distress, making a theory out of it; yet it is also the prose of a prophet and moralist, increasingly so as the 1920s and 1930s wore on. My reaction to it knocks me off balance and links with the response I have described to *Different Trains*; yet once again, it is a discovery, not an intention, and one that always puts the writing in jeopardy just as it breathes life into it. These letters that always reach their destination result in us being called to something, but also, once they are prised open, reveal a great deal about the limits of what we can consciously know about ourselves, and how our writing might take us over and leave us somewhere uncomfortable, but also—I hope—able to discover something new.

Chapter 4

Becoming an author

Martin Weegmann

It so happened that it took me forever and a day to find myself within my voice. To know the true "Martin sound". Maybe this is the case for us all, to know those voices we no longer wish to express, or tone down, and the ones we do wish to voice. Not to mention the new voices and "sounds" we acquire along the way, be those cultural voices, family lore, those acquired through friends, colleagues, teachers, and many others. There's a witty-wise word from Oscar Wilde (note 1), who said that we (or "most people", he qualified) are quotations, made up out of the opinions of others. Whilst there is a grain of truth in this and, however limited in originality, we are, surely, much more than echoes and imitations in the long process of becoming who we are. Narrative therapists call us multi-story creatures, crisscrossed by complicated layers of narratives that are patterned in unique idioms. And so, from speech to writing. Nowadays, I enjoy finding myself in print too, in a written voice. Of all the language roads which we travel (i.e., speaking, hearing, reading, writing), writing is the last to acquire, and, if published, is a committed act in the way in which ordinary speech is not. For me, publishing is about having something to say, with a wider reach, and is a means to share, to address and sometimes to redress issues. I have come to trust in writing, in the sense that I know that words will find me just as much as I search for them; to paraphrase artist Paul Klee, a sentence starts with a word that goes for a walk. And I have learned to "write out" just as one can "speak out". It's a form of catharsis and communication, and has taken fifteen years plus to practise and improve, that and a great amount of reading and noticing what and how others write. I read extensively before then, and wrote much too, but here I am referring to the emergence of a conscious publication desire. I'll share some moments within this period, describing some of the purposes and passions that have spurred me.

Who has been there already?

It's a clumsy expression, but Foucault (1977) said that Freud, alongside a few other notables, was a "founder of discursivity". In other words, he created a vast vocabulary of human, unconscious life that is permanently associated with him. But, famous as he was, Freud knew his originality was limited, in that the poets and philosophers had already visited those sites. "Depth psychology" hardly begins with psychoanalysis, as its nineteenth-century literary sources are, arguably, many. Take a novella such as *Jekyll and Hyde*, written ten years or so before the *Studies in Hysteria*, which brings in all the great themes of man's "double being", the dream and the nightmare, metamorphosis and the operations of the unknown mind. Stevenson was equally influenced by *his* times, including a then fascination with idea of double consciousness, dissociation, and threats to civilisation by the aberrant individual or dangerous classes. In this sense, the figure of Hyde is a great summary individual. Writing remains site visiting, in that no one has any "pure finds" any more.

For me, writing is a form of working-over, or writing-over, in response to new ideas or something over which I am in struggle. I worked for a long time in substance misuse services, and, sustained as I was by a host of influential psychological writings, and a fewer number of psychodynamic ones, found most publications flat and uninspiring, hardly doing justice to nuances and the lived experience of that most devastating of disorders. I understand the reasons for a certain type of writing, in that academic conventions exist for a good purpose, but these can inhibit expression and constrain creativity. Rather by chance, I found compensation for this frustration in coming across the plays of Eugene O'Neill, and was soon inspired to publish my first psychotherapy paper (2002). The intrigue of O'Neill's is not difficult to explain; from an autobiographical point of view, he knew alcoholism and despair, although he did establish sobriety, rather an abstinence from alcohol, without much peace of mind. He once said that writing filled his emptiness, was a "vacation from living". His family was deeply scarred as were, in turn, his own children. Many of his plays are awash with reference to drink and the lifestyle of the tavern. One of his real-world haunts was "the Hell Hole", re-incarnated as the saloon in *The Iceman Cometh*.

I came to learn as much about the tragic mixing of human souls with abandonment to alcohol from literary works as I ever did from drier psychology or psychotherapy papers. This is not to claim that literary approaches are superior, or sufficient in themselves, but they can provide us with a different entrée point, offering rich experiential and imaginative resources. The prompting provided by the literary realm can be remarkable. If, say, one describes depression as "winter within", it vividly conveys something about an awful locked-in feeling, and one of inner cold; similarly, if one refers to the experience of rejection or dejection as the soul having "gone abroad" (Coleridge). In the late seventeenth century, the composer Dowland expresses the experience of melancholy with astonishing beauty in his lyrics, even as it touches violence towards the self;

"Unquiet thoughts, your civil slaughter stint". Poetry, or lyrics, can indeed help us see, "where the meanings are" (Dickinson), but *differently*.

I continue to admire Eugene O'Neill, and, recently, used the play *Anna Christie* to address the formation of what I call "hardened selves" and "roughened lives" (Weegmann, 2016), lives, moreover, that could easily be ours, be anyone's, given the right or the wrong circumstances. Life might have its choices, but is also a chance production. I use the characters in his astonishing play, their dialogue, rather as one might use clinical examples and build theoretical discussion around them. For me, one particular line captures the human fact of contingency and the potential for adversity with admirable economy and disturbing beauty, "We're all poor nuts and things happen, and we just get mixed in wrong, that's all" (O'Neil, 1995, p. 67).

Writing as intervention

Many of my earlier publications were about addiction. They were interventions in the sense that, like a pragmatist philosopher, I wanted to get something *done*. If Pierce was right, that thinkers are not solo beings but are part of a "community of inquirers", then through my work I wanted to create a bridge and forge a better channel of communication. The book, *Psychodynamics of Addiction* (2002), arose from that sort of wish. The two "communities" I had in mind were the world of psychotherapy, on the one hand, which I felt contained a lot of prejudice and often little actual experience with addicted individuals, and the world of substance misuse services, on the other hand, where I found interest in but no obvious training available in psychodynamic understanding. It is likely that this talk of "two communities" was exaggerated and that there were no such coherent partners waiting, ready and eager for dialogue. If only. But, if writing is an act of intervention, then it can also help *create* new connections and partners in thought and practice. One result was, for example, an annual two-day conference, Psychotherapy of Addiction, which I ran with colleagues for eight years.

I still like the intervention metaphor, at least for some purposes. I guess it works best when one tries to transcend worn theories or unserviceable assumptions to advance something new, and which may re-cast the debate. Writing can express and mobilise personal passion, and bring thinking and feeling together, as in the example of my anger with psychotherapy prejudices, as I saw them. A publication, however, still has to be more than an ego-document.

At another juncture, to bring in another example, I witnessed the effects of real-life homophobia on someone. It was truly distressing. I was already aware of troubled history, to say the least, between homosexuality and psychoanalysis, so, I (Weegmann, 2007) excavated that history and considered the role of pernicious (in my view) social prejudices in our professional field, broadly speaking. I also wanted to press my place of training, the Institute of Group Analysis, not to remain on the sidelines, or to rest on comfortable assumptions of "our openness" as compared to, say, "the psychoanalysts" (as if they spoke as one body anyway). It seems to me that whilst analytic institutions have had a lot to say about the nature of reparation in patients, they need the courage to face those areas in which *they* might have got matters wrong and not always well served particular client groups. Writing can, in modest ways, help heal wounds, "writing wrongs".

I not want to romantise "speaking out" ("writing out") as some lone act of heroism. One never acts alone. However, the role of authority (with venerated founders, lines of descent, loyalties) and function of a strong canon (the secular equivalent to a body of work that is "of authority", and which represents *the* standard) in psychoanalysis, can make innovation, let alone proper testing, a fraught and painful venture.

Publication pride

Psychodynamic approaches usually concentrate attention on the role of anxiety as an accompaniment of human experience. In relation to writing, for example, there has been a fair amount written on publication anxiety and oedipal competition, including the famous "anxiety of influence" thesis as initiated by literary critic Harold Bloom (1997). The anxiety generated by thoughts such as "what do *I* have to say?", "how can I justify being in the same journals as my therapist or teachers?", and so forth. "The published" can gain in status and over time may become "big names". In relation to the literary field that Bloom addresses, poets are rendered anxious by the influence of precursor poets, the "poet within the poet" is how he puts it. All of these factors can and do apply, and are ably discussed by other authors in this book. The word "publication" is, to my mind, a wonderfully evocative, semi-sociological term—to make something generally known, to bring to a *public*. To do so, there has to be a professional growing up to the point when one is no longer living under the (direct) apprenticeship, dependence, and shadow of others, other writers, admired figures, hallowed traditions, and so forth. How does one find a voice within a forest already grown? Or move beyond over-reference and deference? All this, together with a preparedness to face the practical magnitude of the task of publication, with its daunting stages and requirements.

There is another side, too, one to which Bloom also directs us, in his latest offering—*The Anatomy of Influence* (2011)—proffered as his "final reflections" on the influence process (well, he has to stop writing at some stage!). Here, he talks of literary *love* and of a subtler language of influence, which, he reminds us, is close in etymology to *inspire*, to breathe life into. Confidence grows as one takes part in publication projects. A measure of pride too, not in any imagined defeat of others, and triumph of competition, but simply for the act of "joining" a published community and in the enjoyment of that achievement. Sontag (2001, p. 224) says that, "Writing is a series of permissions you give yourself to be expressive in certain ways. To invent. To leap." That is how I experience it.

Names in print

By way of comparison, I asked two colleagues to tell me how they experience(d) the move into writing. They speak for themselves. First, a clinical psychology trainee, on the achievement of her first step in publication. She comments:

> with a little embarrassed glow in my cheeks, I enter my name into Google Scholar... it is an exciting moment to see the paper appear, with my name in black solid letters... I feel like I've entered a prestigious club, or the serious world of academics. This is an indelible mark on who I am as a professional, something that will forever be attached to me. Strangers can now search for me too, and make judgments on my stance and opinions before even meeting me. My mind skips forward over a fantasy research-rich career....

Second, an analyst who has published continually throughout a long career. In looking back to recall his first responses to publishing, he spoke about "excitement, tinged with performance anxiety, performance in the sense of needing to demonstrate a skill, and with that the fear of failing". He spoke of the "vulnerability in opening oneself up, and yet there was the ambition too, in stepping up and reaching a wider public readership". Asked how he felt about writing once he had several successful publications under his belt, he commented:

> It got easier, more familiar, thought never easy. I enjoyed working on other people's work, people whom I admired, and that gave me some security. Making connections was the satisfying aspect, not just exposing myself....

The literary mind

What if the mind doesn't write poetry, but *is* poetic? Doesn't create literature, but *is* literary? And the self, not a teller of stories but which *is* those stories. I'm sensitive if people ask me to describe my professional orientation and I don't much like to be classified. But if pushed, I say that I'm somewhere in an arc between the psychodynamic and narrative (and I practise other approaches besides). I've become more and more interested in the latter and am fond of quoting people, like philosopher MacIntyre (1984), "we are story-telling animals"; writers, such as Wilde, "life imitates art"; or psychologist Bruner (1994), with his dramatic statement "no narrative, no self". There is a whole interdisciplinary movement, drawing on cognitive science and other sources, that attests to the notion that human beings are literary-minded. We have literary minds. And life, as reported, really can seem like literature. The interest came gradually, not only in what I read, but in the everyday practice of concentrated listening and reflective responding. I am fascinated by the brilliance with which people, regardless of education, or even of formal literacy, "make their point" and use language (and its pauses) to persuade, argue, insult, appreciate, agree, underscore, hit the jugular, exaggerate, seduce, and a universe of other effects. I recall, with the amusement that time affords, one of my clients who, with admirable verbal skill, exposed my weaknesses as he saw them, "There's only two things that I can fault you on— your listening and your understanding". How to demolish a psychologist in one go!

In philosophy, this touches upon "speech-act" theory, with the emphasis on the *act*, to have an impact in talk. The opening of a mouth can sometimes have truly dramatic effects. This is also true of those who are short of words for emotions and who short-circuit emotional processing by leaping into physical action (self-harm, aggressive acts, etc.); they too, but maybe only after the emotional storm subsides, still have an expressive repertoire, even if one that is blunted or limited to one channel. "Articulate" and "non-articulate" are not, it seems to me, absolute qualities that one either has or does not. The same is true of that other slippery phrase, "psychological mindedness". If psychoanalysis was the "talking cure", then maybe narrative psychology is the conversation that arises by talking about the words we choose. The "putting" is the decisive bit, reflecting as it does the narrativised version of the self and world that we create. We live "under descriptions" of ourselves, says Hacking. Words can box experience, and our hexed problems, our habitual "ways of putting things", keep us, well, just that, problem-bound. As human beings, we can sentence ourselves.

The written word, the "writing act", can have a place in psychotherapy too....

Letters

I began asking clients to write letters addressing their problems, giving them a piece of paper with only the word "Dear....". They were to do the rest, to decide what to write, in what style, and to decide on the nature of the communication (I try not to influence the content, for example by suggesting it should necessarily be a "good-bye" letter), and to sign off in a way they feel most fitting. For those who struggle with literacy, or who are self-conscious (many apologise for spelling, for example), I offer to write for them, as they speak. It can be done within the session, or in the time between sessions. Letters like these are commonly used in narrative therapy, and in some other approaches (such as CAT), and, as unplannable, imaginative procedures, are a remarkable in-road to understanding more about a person's relationship with their sufferings. I began years ago, with letters to drugs and alcohol, but developed as my experience expanded. "Dear black cloud", "Dear uneventful life", "Dear divorce", and "Dear recovery", are a few more recent examples. Re-authoring is the technical term used, literally "to author again". It is an externalising activity, which I explain to clients as a way of seeing oneself, one's feelings, "out there", in black and white. People are usually surprised, often moved by what they write. And I have learned over and over that one can never predict what occurs. Letters are rich, descriptive resources, constituting a "live document".

Although the practice of writing to clients is meant to be (more) standard in (NHS) mental health, more often than not, when done, it is sent to a fellow professional, with the client copied in. But what if it were the other way around, that we write to the client and copy in the professional? Therapeutic letters of this sort, to clients, are an altogether different art. I was first encouraged to try this when working at the Henderson therapeutic community, a good place in which power relations, including those of clients and professionals (indeed, those invested with authority to write reports), could be contested or equalised. Subsequently, I treated such letters as drafts, to be shared with the client, who might then wish to edit or modify the content, until an agreed form of words arrived. I often include poems, or quotations from ancient wisdom, if I think it will reach something that could not be put in any better way. In a recovery group on an acute ward, for example, we collected "favourite sayings" and "wise reminders" that patients could offer, both as words to self, and to fellows. I included myself in this, sharing examples of words that helped me out during difficult times. Like that of a Native American poem:

> When you are in doubt, be still, and wait. When doubt no longer exists for you, then go forward with courage. So long as mists envelop you, be still. Be still until the sunlight pours through and dispels the mists—as it surely will; Then act with courage.
>
> (attributed to Chief White Eagle, Ponca)

All the same, writing, once sent or published, is unalterable. Epston (1994) makes the point that conversation is ephemeral, and whilst it may be powerful at the time, its detail is quickly lost. Letters, by contrast, "don't fade". The conversation is extended. Letters can be quoted and read, months and years after the event.

Writing and the extended self

Many people think with a pen (or the modern equivalent). Funny how helpful such a little thing is. But William James was right, that life is full of such extended dimensions of the "me" and "mine", so that an author has "my books", "my readers", "my publisher", "my next book", and so on.

As relevant to writing, the "self" is extended in terms of space (e.g., in the journal, the library, the catalogue, the reading list), and time (e.g., early work, collected papers, anticipated next book). If the writing in question happens to be life writing (e.g., *mémoires*, autobiography, diaries, letters), the self is extended as a sort of personal archive and potential legacy, that may, if the person is sufficiently famous, echo down the decades, or longer.

I think it was Gertrude Stein who said that we write for ourselves and for strangers, to which I would add, also for our peers, our group. So, reflecting on to whom I write, as well the satisfaction of working something out for myself, I do seek the wider audience of others in the broad fields of psychology and psychotherapy (I identify with both professional groupings), the strangers, and my "imagined peers", who may or may not read what I have produced (including a circle of people I actually know presently, and others with whom, say, I once trained, or might once have worked with) and, finally, friends, who might (I trust!) read me either regularly, from time to time, or just appreciate the fact that they know it means a lot to me. There is an achievement aspect, work already done, and an aspiration aspect, the work I hope to do in the future, about which I may or may not have explicit plans.

Why write, again?

At its simplest, I write when I have something that I judge important to say. The feelings that propel the writing might be strong—did not Sartre (1950) describe writing as the "taking of positions"? Writing passions and purposes are intertwined, although, depending on the context and nature of the publication (e.g., an academic journal), what is personal to it may be kept well out of sight. Without personal passion, however, there is no reason to write at all. The readership I have in mind is hardly neutral, as I seek an audience who will bear witness to my purpose, and who may be influenced, persuaded, challenged, and so forth. I finish with two recent examples around the elusive writing question.

A paper that I co-wrote (Weegmann & Head, 2016) explores the help that can be provided for the "family and friends" of those with mental health disorders, entitled "circles of care". I feel for such people and fought hard to set up new groups in several services that could help address their needs. "Family and friends" are people on the edges of services, supporting other people who are themselves on other margins, in this case those with substance misuse or personality disorder. I can talk about *how* my interest arose more easily than *why*, and have not been in a similar position myself; the nearest I came, and here only maybe, was witnessing my father's long descent due to Alzheimer's disease, although I was neither his carer nor was I living at home at the time. More likely, such identifications are learned during the course of professional life and connect with strong, motivating values. In my case, I've always felt an identification with those who are marginalised, or who lack a voice, and as a professional I like to create innovative spaces in the services with whom I work. Equally, I enjoy innovative writing.

Friends and family experience considerable hardship and are disempowered by cumulative negative events, feelings of powerlessness, self-criticism, shame, threats, and many others. Family members risk deterioration in their physical and psychological wellbeing from the stresses of living with such difficulties, their relationships skewed and roles are distorted. From start to finish, the paper took just over a year. Patience is required, in the lengthy process from the germ of an idea, to numerous drafts, peer review, and all the other requirements of journal submission. It got there in the end, and attracted positive commentary, which was gratifying. It was noticed.

Finally, in a book chapter (Weegmann, 2017), I addressed some aspects of Palestinian experience, a chapter that was as painful to compose as it felt necessary. The edited book is about the "social unconscious" in societies, and so I wrote to the editors, concerned that there might be no place for those living in devastated societies, those with no security or boundaries, no place for a people marked by chronic exclusion and rightlessness. Fortunately, they were persuaded, and so I granted myself "permission to narrate", to borrow a phrase from Said, who writes of systematic efforts to reduce Palestinian existence. Palestinians reduced to invisibility, conjured away, or allowed the negative appearance of cameo figures within a grander play (that of Israel), only ever and intractability associated with margins, nuisance, and violence.

The exemplary writer and poet Mahmoud Darwish knew how to articulate experience of societal suffering and ever-prolonged displacement. My chapter uses some of his poetic references to attest to a reality that is deeply uncomfortable and hard to classify. I use his phrase "after the last sky", in the chapter title. In situations of massive social trauma, with ongoing occupation and removal, there are always levels of knowing and non-knowing, and literary and metaphorical resources provide one of the ways in which such realities can be defended against oblivion. When Darwish (2003, p. 11) wrote, "We travel like everyone else, but we return to nothing. Ours is a country of words" ("We Travel Like All People"), he underscores the remarkably thin and precarious nature of Palestinian existence. Addressing this fragility was a life mission, hence the obligation, stated in the same poem, to speak out, to "Talk, Talk". Fearless and sensitive talk, and in this case in the written form, is essential.

I had corresponded with the late George Awad, a Palestinian psychoanalyst who lived in Toronto, a few years earlier. I said that I felt awkward, as a British person, to presume to write about a people far away, with whom I have no connections, but about whom I have long been interested. He replied that everyone is far away if we place them so. All writers need their interlocutors. My Palestine chapter honours his encouragement.

And so?

Every stopping point is a choice, and I have no singular conclusion about writing and authorship with which to finish. Only that I have offered a few backscatterings upon what draws me on as a writer. Finding one's style requires practice, a lot of it, and which develops every time one tries. As for this project, editing a book on writing clearly says something about my passion in the subject. I experience delight in seeing what comes in from the writers who are part of this project. I enjoy creating, in this case co-creating, finding new ground and inviting others into the project, a group-in-print. Sartre made the point that whereas, say, the shoemaker can try on shoes he makes, the writer cannot be the reader. That involves others, and one has to wait. Hence, the question of where this project will "go" as a completed book expresses an uncertainty about outcomes that I do not control, but the readers (and reviewers) do, or at least more so.

> Most people are other people. Their thoughts are someone else's opinions, their lives a mimicry, their passions a quotation.
>
> Oscar Wilde

Chapter 5

Mad desire and feverish melancholy

Reflections on the psychodynamics of academic writing

Nick Barwick

Introduction

A few years ago, the night I agreed to write a keynote paper, I had a dream.

> I was preparing to go out for the evening—a significant party or social occasion. My wife and some friends were downstairs. I was upstairs in the bathroom shaving, trimming my beard. I wanted to make sure the cut was sharp, clean. Yet when I looked in the mirror, what I saw was that, somehow, I had managed to shave off the left half of my beard, leaving the white flesh entirely exposed. At that moment, startled by both my vulnerability and ridiculousness, I realised it was time to go downstairs and "meet the public". I awoke with feelings of intense anxiety and the fear of terrible humiliation and shame.

This dream, despite the passing years, still captures something of the profound anxiety that, even now, can seize me when writing. All the "realities" I try to bring to bear; a literary background, long experience as an editor, a published track record, successful pedagogic and therapeutic work with many writers, both student and professional, struggling with writing blocks, feel no more than "fragments ... shored against my ruin" (Eliot, 1922). Instead, the dream-image prevails, a reflection that prompts in me, now as then, a desire to decline the proffered writing space and instead withdraw. Such withdrawal promises immediate relief but also loss; not least the lost opportunity to share and create. Such a loss and the willingness to bear that loss are predicated, at least in part, I believe, upon the difficulty in bearing other losses, both prior and potential—in particular, a "loss of face".

This phrase, so often casually employed, speaks much. It speaks, for example, of a loss of courage—an inability to "face up to" or "face down" what lies ahead. It speaks of humiliation, of having one's face rubbed in it, where "it" is the shitty reality—often as much our own as others' making—that inevitably, "let's face it", bruises our narcissistic dreams.

It speaks also of the feared loss of self, both the protective "false self"—as in "put on a face"—and, beneath what is put on, the exposed "true self": the face which, for most of us, is that aspect of our bodies which we believe most nearly expresses the core of who we are. There is much, then, at stake in a "loss of face".

In this brief preamble, already I am aware of throwing rather a lot into the case I am trying to make—or should I say, pack—about anxieties inherent in writing and, in particular, academic writing. Indeed, I am reminded of a passage from Michael Ondaatje's *Anil's Ghost*:

> When he wrote, he slipped into the page as if it were water, and tumbled on. The writer was a tumbler ... If not, then a tinker, carrying a hundred pots and pans and bits of linoleum and wires and falconer's hood and pencils and ... you carried them around for years and gradually fit them into a small, modest book. The art of packing.
>
> (Ondaatje, 2000)

I should now like to unpack some of the pots and pans I've been tumbling for the last few pages, and indeed for the last good few years.

A Kleinian pot

The defence I nearly chose or, more accurately, felt impelled to chose, against this feared "loss of face"—that is, of identity, of all that I am, would like to, and feel that I should, be—was "withdrawal". Carrying as it does both military and sexual connotations, this word betrays a myriad fears and phantasies. In both semantic fields, it denotes a *pre*-caution, the strategic intention of which is to prevent full-frontal engagement. To engage, it is feared, is to instigate a catastrophic birth-cum-slaughter.

The link between creativity and aggression, and the losses that need to be borne in the struggle to develop and give birth to something new, are central to Kleinian thought, and it was in the guise of a Kleinian t(h) inker that I explored some of what I thought to be the reasons for essay anxiety some years ago (Barwick, 1995, 2000).

My explorations took as their premise an analogy: that the texts from which students read prior to producing their own texts/essays could be likened to the mother. The transition from consumer to producer was only fully possible, I suggested, if the student is able to bear the loss of the "mother text", or more accurately, bear its transformation, since the text produced has to be born out of the digested parts of the text (or texts) consumed. Tolerance of the transformation and the loss it implies is complicated by the aggressive nature of the feeding and digestion processes. Students need to "get their teeth" into a text. They must "enter into it", "pull it to pieces", make it their own. Such creative use of aggression may bring succour of personalised knowledge, yet phantasies arising from unconscious recognition of aggression's destructive nature may also bring anxieties of guilt (Joseph, 1978; Klein, 1935).

I went on to suggest that how aggression is experienced depends upon the experience of containment (Bion, 1962); my hypothesis being that many students, gripped by the intellectual paralysis resulting from essay anxiety, were haunted by phantasies arising from uncontained feelings of aggression.

To add to the infantile phantasies stirred up by the prospect and act of essay-writing, I suggested adolescent-oriented phantasies also played their part, since, as the body acquires adult potency, curiosity and its ally, independent, creative, original thought, are not only aggressive but sexualised. Indeed, the Hebrew word for knowledge—*da'at*—is rooted in sex. Thus, phantasies about "entering", "devouring", "knowing" the text and then conceiving an essay may, at an unconscious level, give rise to disturbing phantasies about parental jealousy, envy, and retribution. This, after all, is how it was for the first adolescents. Adam and Eve, feeding from the Tree of Knowledge—committing thereby both original thought and sin—first became excited, then fearful, then ashamed. Fearful, they hid from the Father. To some degree, of course, the fear was worse than the reality. Although innocent dependence *was* lost, Adam and Eve were neither destroyed nor entirely abandoned. They were, however, humbled, made mortal, and exiled from the parental home.

An oedipal pot

This story of the Fall reminds me of another tale of coupling and collapse:

> And they said, Go to, let us build us a city and a tower, whose top may reach unto heaven: and let us make us a name, lest we be scattered abroad upon the face of the whole earth.
>
> And the Lord came down to see the city and the tower, which the children of men builded.
>
> And the Lord said, Behold, the people is one, and they have all one language; and this they begin to do: and now nothing will be restrained from them, which they have imagined to do.
>
> Go to, let us go down, and there confound their language, that they may not understand another's speech.
>
> So the lord scattered them abroad from thence upon the face of the earth: and they let off to build the city.
>
> (Genesis 11: 4–8)

In both the Eden and the Tower of Babel stories, people "get it together" and are punished for doing so. These tales could be read as warnings against omnipotence. The all-knowing Father, firmly but wisely, puts his children in their place. Alternatively, they could be the acts of a "jealous (indeed, envious) God", one who, enraged by the threat of displacement, divides the over-excitable aspirants and, by dint respectively of mortal blow and ruined tower, cuts them down to an appropriately diminutive size.

It is often difficult to assess whether the actions and/or words of a "third", which have the effect of frustrating our possession of the good object, are prompted by destructive envy or good intent. Indeed, even when we do trust the good intent, the frustration may be so great, the blow to our dream so wounding, we cannot bear it, or them. (The fate of the messenger who bears bad tidings is well known.)

Hannah Segal (1989) suggests that it is the frustration at the breast that causes the infant to split off the bad aspects and with them create a proto-type third. This third grows in complexity as the containers available for such projections become more plentiful: first, part objects—bad breast, penis—then whole objects partially construed—father, mother—and finally, any object, animate or inanimate, that fits the bill: the critic, the essay assessor, the essay itself. An adequate experience of containment helps to modify such splitting and projection; an inadequate experience does not. In this case, the "third", whatever the guise, is ever more likely to be perceived as threat. Unable to bear the frustration with which its presence is associated, we continually seek to ban it—to exclude it from our company. Such exiles, of course, bear both real and projected grudges and are the perfect vehicles of both phantasised and real ret-ribution. Meanwhile, enamoured of our own company and temporar-ily swollen by our own omnipotent, masturbatory phantasies, either we continue to build our towers, blind to imminent danger, or, trembling with persecutory guilt, try all manner of shifty convolutions to hide our shame.

There is, of course, in the end, nowhere to hide. This is because every creative act of coupling, by its very nature, both excludes and produces a third, and this third, whether cast in the role of god or terrorist, sees all, since it lives within us as well as without. Thus, while it is in coupling that we seek succour, at some point we must face a fact well known to proverbial wisdom: that things happen in threes.

Oedipal illusions

Sigmund Freud, in "Mourning and melancholia" (1917e), links sanity (essentially the individual's capacity to stay in touch with reality) to the capacity to give up the idea of a permanent possession of the loved ob-ject. Melanie Klein develops this notion (1935, 1940), noting that from the moment of weaning, we are called upon to relinquish possession of aspects of the external world, over which we have limited or no control. Out of such relinquishment, out of the frustration of our deepest desire and expectations, we may, if our envy is not too great, learn to install what is lost in the external world in our internal, psychic one.

The oedipal situation is inextricably bound up in the issue of loss since, when our desired, dreamt-of object is absent (and thus lost to us), there is an important sense in which it may be understood to be elsewhere—that is, with a third. This is never easy to acknowledge and certainly, at some level, is experienced as a profound blow to our narcissism. Yet, if we are to mature—that is, to develop in a real way our relationship with the world, which includes our relationships with of our loved objects—then we must be willing to witness and able to tolerate the loved object's possession by another. Arguing along these lines, Ronald Britton (1985) proposes that the question at the core of a healthy negotiation of the oedipal situation is "will our love survive knowledge?" (p. 45), particularly our growing awareness of the separateness of our love objects and their relationships with others which exclude us? If our doubts are greater than our faith in this respect, we are likely to take refuge in "the cultivation of illusions", amongst which the oedipal illusion in which the phantasy of remaining the secret chosen one is often favoured.

For some students, I suggest, the essay itself represents the unwanted third, from which an internal coupling of student and "mother text", or the imagined produce of that coupling, is kept secret. This is not surprising since the form of the academic essay itself has a natural valency for negative projections. Characteristically involving an accepted code of terminology appropriate to its subject orientation, a tightly organised argument, a series of apt exempla, framed by opening and concluding generalities (all of which are of course to be duly scrutinised by yet another third, the reader-cum-hard-marker), its demands are great.

> Kevin frequently found he could do little more than begin essays. They often petered out after a couple of paragraphs. He described this experience as if "all the life goes out of it"—"it" being the ideas with which he began each essay venture. He described the essay form as "insensitive", "ungiving", and the organisation and planning the essay required as "uncreative". "To be honest", he added, "I don't want to give my feelings up to it. They'd get lost."

Kevin's attitude to the essay can be seen in terms of the devouring container. The written word itself had this characteristic for him. Yet I think it is useful to think about his essay anxiety in terms of the intolerable third. From this perspective, he cannot bear to share the good object he possesses with another, for fear that that "other" will rob him of all potency. His defence is to hide.

One further extended example I would like to give captures, I think, the nature of some of the oedipal anxieties which can so confound a student's efforts to begin writing. It's a vignette about Harry.

Harry was a young would-be writer of eleven. Although intelligent and eager to write, he appeared almost totally unable to maintain concentration in class. While others worked, he would soon start fiddling: with books, with pencils, with anything to hand. This included the belongings of those around him. It was the disruption that this led to that led Harry to Anne, a counsellor-trained, special needs teacher who I was supervising.

The first thing Harry said when he came into Anne's room was, "So this is what my mum's room looks like!" Harry's mum, who Anne met later to discuss Harry's progress, was a special needs assistant. She was a drawn, tired-looking woman, committed to her job, who would not, despite Harry's protests and evident interest, tell him anything about her work on the grounds of "confidentiality". She told Anne what an exhausting child Harry was and had always been. Indeed, as a baby he had cried so much that neither she nor her husband got a wink of sleep. Consequently, she had moved out of her own room so as not to disturb her husband. Enquiring about Harry's relationship with his father, Harry's mother said it was "difficult", confirming Harry's own experience, summed up by the fact that his father, no matter how hard Harry tried, always called him "stupid".

Harry worked well with Anne. He caught up with much missed work. Yet despite this, his behaviour in class did not improve.

Anne's room was situated on the upper part of a split-level room, the lower, larger part being dedicated to music lessons. These music lessons often took place while Anne worked with individual children. Harry, having already had a number of writing-focused sessions without any musical activities taking place below, was, for the first time, forced to witness just such a "scene".

What happened was that while Harry was concentrating at work, Anne left him a while and went over to look at the music class below. A moment later, she became aware of Harry standing next to her. In a tone heavy with contempt, he said, "I feel really sorry for you." Anne asked why. Harry answered with a question, "Don't *you* just want to drop something on top of them?" Anne asked if he hated music. "No", he replied. "I love music. I just can't stand anyone else *making it*, while I'm not."

Two morals, I think, can be drawn from this story. The first is that to write (indeed, to engage in any kind of sustained process of creative symbolisation), it is necessary to be able to have faith and take pleasure in the creative act of coupling. To write, writers must engage and couple with their own internal objects and with the essentially external object of the written word. The second moral is that these capacities—to have faith and be able to take pleasure in the act of coupling—are dependent upon having borne witness to such acts of coupling. To "bear" witness is an apt collocation, since what must be tolerated is a sense of one's own exclusion.

The dynamics of Harry's family suggest an environment unsuited for lessons in this kind of witness training. Here, coupling becomes a source of envy as much as of aspiration, whilst exclusion, far from being tolerated, gives rise to retributive acts. Thus the infant Harry, in claiming his mother, divides his parents, breeding resentment in both. This resentment is played out by a parallel exclusion of Harry by his mother from her work and repeated acts of retribution by a father who appears compelled to castrate any glimmers of creativity in Harry's mind.

Ronald Britton describes the import of such oedipal transactions in the development of the epistemophilic impulse:

> The primal family triangle provides the child with two links connecting him separately with each parent and confronts him with the link between them which excludes him ... If the link between the parents perceived in love and hate can be tolerated in the child's mind, it provides him with a prototype for an object relationship of a third kind in which he is a witness and not a participant. A third position then comes into existence from which object relationships can be observed. Given this, we can also envisage *being* observed. This provides us with a capacity for seeing ourselves in interaction with others and for entertaining another point of view whilst retaining our own, for reflecting on ourselves whilst being ourselves.
>
> (Britton, 1989, p. 87)

Such a capacity is what we hope of patients-cum-clients in therapy—the ability to maintain a therapeutic split constituted of "observing" and "experiencing" ego (Sterba, 1934) and, through this, to engage with us in a therapeutic alliance. It is also this ability, I believe, that is central in enabling students to write essays.

Oedipal dis-illusions and the writing alliance

"There are three rules for writing", said Somerset Maugham. "Unfortunately, no one knows what they are." This perfectly encapsulates the curious paradox experienced by the writer, that there is a right way of doing it but that that right way has to be rediscovered each time.

When I was eleven, a new teacher was a little less enigmatic. He asked the class to open the front cover of our exercise books and to write there the three things that were the essential components of all good writing. They were:

1   Some paper
2   A pen
3   Myself

I think a sense of omnipotence is vital in the act of creation. Without it, nothing begins. Yet the loss of the beloved object—the possession of that perfect piece I have in mind—must be borne. And not just once, but again and again and again. To write, says J.-B. Pontalis, is both to dream and to mourn:[1]

> to be animated by a mad desire to possess things through language, and to experience with each page, sometimes with each word, that this is never it! Hence the feverishness and melancholy, sometimes the one, sometimes the other, that always accompany the act of writing.
>
> (1993, p. xviii)

Further, during these fumbled acts of never quite satisfactory coupling, as feeling becomes thought and thought becomes word and word becomes phrase and sentence and paragraph and page, we must be able both to engage fully, to abandon ourselves wholeheartedly, painfully, and pleasurably, and yet retain a sense of perspective from which we can bear witness to the loss, tolerate the frustrating exclusion bound up in that loss, and face the gap between what we have and what we desire.

Writing under the influence

In *The Anxiety of Influence* (1973), the literary critic Harold Bloom describes the difficulties a writer faces when he fears that a "dominant predecessor" has "already taken total possession of the field" (Britton, 1997, p. 18). I first came across Bloom's thesis as an undergraduate when, disappearing under the weight of literary criticism which I felt it incumbent upon me to read before ever venturing an opinion of my own, I told myself that if I did not risk writing "something that was me", I would not write at all. As I came across Bloom again in preparing this paper—Britton (1997) refers to him in a chapter on "publication anxiety" (revised and extended in Britton, 1998)—I too felt the anxiety of influence. Britton has contributed significantly to my thinking in this paper and, on re-reading some of his work in the process of preparation, it struck me how present his influence is in some of my previous writing on essay anxiety and how much, therefore, I find myself in his debt. My awareness of such debt is a cause of both anxiety and consolation: consolation in that, having a good role model to draw on, I do not feel so out on a limb; anxiety because I find myself fearing the humiliation I may receive for seeking, by means fair or foul, to possess knowledge already possessed.

I note with a certain amusement (at least that self-reflective witness within me does) that my mention of my first encounter with Bloom as an undergraduate might be aptly interpreted by Britton as a "distraction".

My effort to claim authority in the face of a feared diminishing space in which to make my mark, leads me to digress. Britton analyses a number of distractions, distortions, and digressions in people's writing as they struggle to negotiate the nature of their oedipal relationships with eminent forebears. These include some interesting asides from Karl Abraham (1924) as at first he challenges, then defers, then challenges again the prevailing paradigm (that is, Freud's) regarding melancholia. Such convolutions are symptomatic of an inner oedipal conflict: the desire to possess the good object and the fear of the excluded third (and his or her allies) who previously possessed it; the desire to express one's debt and the desire to come into one's own. Such a struggle for *auth*ority, for *auth*enticity, is the very stuff that *auth*orial individuation is made on.

The delusion that sometimes besets some authors is that either they are Author of All (that is, God) or author of nothing, when truth is, what we may realistically be, is authors of something. As Donald Winnicott remarks, "it is not possible to be original except on a basis of tradition" (1967, p. 117). I think, in a more provocative way, this is what Roland Barthes (1977) alludes to when, challenging the outright possession of texts, he promotes an alternative in the form of "intertextuality": that inextricable interweaving of mind within mind, text within text, like a communal orchestration in which it is difficult to delineate precisely either an end or a beginning. It is within this intertextuality (one that is charged with oedipal anxieties) that the author needs to negotiate a place they can call their own.

> In a group which met without formal agenda but with the sole purpose of reflecting on difficulties experienced in writing publishable papers, three disparate conversations arose. The first centred around how much theory to include; the second on anxieties concerning confidentiality; the third, on how to bring together a mass of research involving detailed interviews with many individuals, in a way that did justice to the individuals, yet allowed the would-be author to establish her own voice.

This third topic, I think, crystallised an important aspect of the other two. "Gaining knowledge of an object", says Britton, "engenders in the individual a sense of possessing it" (Britton, 1997, p. 16). Thus, in the bid to make public that gain—that is, publish—these would-be authors were beset by two dominant, inter-related phantasies and their concomitant anxieties: the feared destruction of the good object aggressively devoured and the feared retribution of a third, be it in the form of suing client or derisive reader-cum-editor-cum-peer-review.

Withdrawal revisited: a Winnicottian perspective

Sometimes, the thought of the external third produces such fear in the would-be writer and stimulates the persecuting internal third so greatly, the writer is forced, for the sake of authenticity and creativity, to cut all ties with the real world. It is as if this oedipal defence of "turning a blind eye" (Steiner, 1985) becomes necessary for creative survival. Such a defensive manoeuvre, however, though often in the short term successful, can leave much to chance. Further, when reality does at last impinge, it can do so with a vengeance.

> Sergei, a professor of composition, was no novice to having his work performed. When he was asked by the conservatoire at which he taught to compose a piece for a centennial celebration, he quickly began writing it. While doing so, he found himself taking enormous compositional risks, including orchestrating on a grand scale. With the piece completed and rehearsals of the various orchestral sections under way, he woke up one night with a panic attack. It suddenly occurred to him that he did not know if the full orchestra (which was to meet for the first time after the weekend) would fit on the stage. He thus spent the whole weekend crawling around the stage with a tape measure, obsessively planning and re-planning the seating permutations.

Sergei's anxiety was caused by the sudden realisation—one he had turned a blind eye to until the night of the dream—that amongst the audience would be his colleagues and his students. What was at stake, he said, was his "authority". Ironically, faced with the possibility that his grandly orchestrated piece would not fit its receptacle, he was suddenly faced with his worst fear: that he would be ridiculed as an "amateur" and thus lose his authority.

It might be argued that Sergei delineated a transitional space for himself, in which the necessary illusion of control, without the impingements of reality (the demands of an external third), allowed him to write. However, the manner in which reality suddenly broke in on him has more a sense of traumatic weaning about it—of an infant, from his mother's breast "untimely (or perhaps just in the nick of time) ripp'd"—than of transition.

As a teacher, I sometimes encouraged students to create what is more akin, I think, to a transitional writing space to place alongside the academic essay. This often took the form of a personal journal. In this space, the writer could take refuge from the impingements of academic demands. Here is an example of a writer, a postgraduate student in his late twenties, using such a journal:

> I am sick. That is where I'll start from. I must give myself a little time for that. Time though is against me ... I have six weeks to finish my dissertation: to write my dissertation, because what I've written I do not own ... So what's the problem?
>
>   It can't be what I've not read, not with the stack of books I've piled beside me. It can't be the lack of notes—I've got over two hundred pages of those. What it is, is a lack of me. Where am I amongst all these words which aren't mine?

A day later, he continues:

> I need an image, an idea—space. I need a space in which to play around. That isn't easy with the pressures I feel. Pressure of time. Pressures of authority. Space, play—these promote meaning, meaning through ownership, possession. They allow me to take in, digest, re-create. Such space occurs only where there is safety, trust, room for encounter, room to move, trip, stumble, get up again. Authority prevents such trust, disallows such space or the playfulness that takes place within it. Just to consider it [authority] makes me hesitate; it makes me distrust my own uncertain being; it makes me think that every utterance is either simplistic, worthless, or mere indulgence. Somehow I must break free. Change the relationship—refuse authority. More precisely, I must make my own.

The writing in this journal is solipsistic. Yet it is also, increasingly, reflective. In this "potential space" (Winnicott, 1971), the lost good object is first recaptured, then played with until, finally, the writer recaptures the capacity to bear witness to the playing. Once this internal triadic relationship—the object of possession, the playful possessor, the witness to the playful possession—is healthily re-established, more academic language can begin to be tolerated within the mental space constituted by its triangulated frame. After a week, the journal begins to peter out. After a fortnight, it is gone. The transition is made back to the academic essay but now with a sense of ownership (based on an intimate coupling) as well as an appropriate sense of debt.

  The temporary withdrawal to the space that the journal represents in this example is not so much a defensive manoeuvre as a tactical one: a chance to re-gather, to re-form before returning to the fray. This is a Winnicottian (1958) view of "withdrawal": a healthy retreat into a state in which objects are subjectively related to and in which, free from traumatic impingements, a sense of feeling "real" can be maintained. Further, it is a temporary

retreat from "the conflict between subjectivity and objectivity and its evocation of the Oedipal situation with its inevitable concomitants of anxiety,
betrayal, guilt and shame" (Britton, 1997, pp. 12–13).

Conclusion/Deadline

The novelist Maggie Gee, when asked how she knew when a piece was
finished, replied: "When the publisher asks for it" (Gee, 1988). I found
myself in something of a similar position as the deadline for presenting
the paper upon which this chapter is based drew inexorably closer. A
quick word count at the end of the first draft revealed a length of over ten
thousand words. This confirmed a fact, I'm happy to say, I was already
aware of—that such an orchestration was far too big to fit onto its allot-
ted stage. The onus was thus on me to cut *myself* down to size.

Such cuts as the "deadline" approaches—that scythe that harbingers
the fateful knowledge of all things neither said nor done—though potentially compromising a paper's weightiness, may make, perhaps, for a
leaner product and one likely to be that bit more digestible. What is more
digestible, of course, is less likely, on the part of the reader, to cause indi-
gestion and, on the part of the writer, less likely to leave the impression
of being full of wind.

This last flatulent metaphor reminds me of one final "fragment" I
would like to proffer. I think it neatly captures a crucial aspect of writing
anxiety by making explicit the link between, on the one hand, potency
of mind (and of the written word) and, on the other, both genital and
anal exertions. Together, genital and anal exertions offer, I think, useful
blueprints for understanding both the excitement and potential shame
involved in presentation and performance anxiety. My suggestion is that,
as the private (that which, at a primitive level, is experienced as being en-
shrined in the body) is made public, the presence of a third, if perceived
as persecutory, is likely to be experienced as reducing sexual precocity to
an act of anal exhibitionism.

And the fragment I spoke of? It takes the form of a vignette:

> A postgraduate student, due to submit a paper, has an anxiety dream
> the night before. In the dream, he finds himself lying outstretched
> in the bath. Standing over him is his wife's best friend, with whom
> he has, in reality, a flirtatious relationship. He watches her looking
> down at him with evident pleasure. He too feels excited, aroused. As
> he bathes in the adoration of her gaze, he becomes aware of voices
> from below, reminding him that wife, family and some friends are
> gathered, waiting to go out for the evening. Suddenly, he feels full
> of wind and, uncontrollably, from between his legs, bubbles start
> rising. He awakes with an overwhelming sense of shame.

This dream, in a number of ways, bears a striking resemblance to my own which I presented at the beginning of this chapter. I hasten to add, however, to save yourself, as reader-cum-witness, embarrassment and to save myself more exposure than is necessary, this particular dream is not mine. Nevertheless, it seems to me that it summarises a number of anxieties regarding writing that might be aptly, if crudely, captured in the feared accusation, "You're writing/talking out of your backside!"

My hope is that this chapter has not been experienced as being too full of wind. Further, though the recalcitrant size of its orchestration undoubtedly betrays anxieties as yet unresolved, I hope I have managed to contain enough of them, particularly those regarding a third, to welcome you, the reader, as witness to this text and not to elicit the turning of a blind eye. As witness, no doubt you will have your own emotional response to what I have said, some of which, I believe, will have its source in your own experience of exclusion. And yet, my hope is that I have revealed enough of the pleasures and pains of my own experience of the process of creative coupling for you to wish and be able to take whatever aspects of this chapter seem most fruitful and, in so doing, gain due pleasure in celebrating your own acts of inter-textual coupling, here and elsewhere.

Note

1 I allude here to J.-B. Pontalis's (1993) description of writing as a process in which the writer is caught in a cycle of dreaming and mourning.

Chapter 6

Clinical writing and the analyst's subjectivity

Laurence Spurling

In a lecture given in 1916, Freud declared to his audience of medical students that whereas they can learn about medicine by watching their teachers in action, "the talk of which psycho-analytic treatment consists brooks no listener; it cannot be demonstrated" (Freud, 1916, p. 17). This is a consequence of the patient's intense and intimate "emotional attachment" to the doctor, which would be disrupted if a third party were to observe the analysis. And so, he told his audience, you cannot be present at a psychoanalytic treatment; you can only really know about it "by hearsay".

The position of the contemporary analytic student and practitioner may seem very different. Students now have a training analysis, giving them first-hand experience of how their personal analyst or therapist works. There is also available a growing body of taped and video-taped psychoanalytic material. However, being a patient and allowing oneself to become dependent and therefore be helped in a personal analysis depends on the student giving up on the kind of critical and discursive thinking and observing which is a necessary part of learning through formal instruction or in clinical supervision. And there is little evidence that the recording of analytic sessions has had much impact on the way psychoanalysis (taken in its widest sense to mean all forms of analytic work) is taught. And so it remains the case that most analytic practitioners will graduate from their training having never seen any of their teachers actually doing psychoanalytic work. They are still having to rely "on hearsay".

Nevertheless, since Freud's lecture the quantity and quality of this "hearsay" has developed enormously. There is now a wide-ranging and rich library of case studies and clinical accounts in the psychoanalytic literature. Given the absence of any first-hand experience of analytic work, these accounts play a very important role in the training and development of analytic practitioners. They function as what the literature on craft practice calls "exemplars", which consist of "a repertoire of examples, images, understandings and actions" (Schoen, 1999, p. 138; Spurling, 2015, p. 81). But given the vast number of clinical accounts that now exist, how does the clinician decide which should serve as examples of good practice? What turns a particular clinical account into an exemplar? Is it simply by virtue of being written by an analytically authoritative or seminal figure? Or is it something more intrinsic to the writing itself—but if so, what?

What is clinical writing trying to do?

In trying to determine what constitutes good clinical writing, we need first to agree on what its function is. Why do analysts write about their work? Freud was clear that in writing his case histories, he was providing backing or evidence for the validity of his theories. In the introduction to the Dora case, for example, he refers to his theoretical ideas on "the pathogenesis of hysterical symptoms", and then asserts that he was proposing "to *substantiate* those views by giving a detailed report of the history of a case and its treatment" (Freud, 1905e, p. 7, italics added). This use of clinical writing as a way of validating one's theoretical ideas figures in the writing of some of the seminal psychoanalytic figures. For example, Melanie Klein writes in the introduction to her "Narrative of a Child Analysis" that "the details of this analysis *clarify* and *support* my concepts" (Klein, 1961, p. 11, italics added). One can note that clarification and support are not the same, but the latter, like Freud's "substantiation", means using the clinical case as a form of validation of one's ideas. This way of using clinical writing has been strongly criticised, both from outside the analytic tradition (e.g., Grunebaum, 1984) and from within (e.g., Spence, 1984), and is now largely discredited within the analytic community. The basic problem is that the analyst is not a neutral or objective observer of the interaction being described but, on the contrary, a necessary participant in the process. Furthermore, this analytic process depends on the establishment of an analytic setting, which is constituted and maintained by the analyst's way of conducting the analysis. The analyst is therefore both participant and designer of the process in which he or she is taking part. In describing his experience of listening to the clinical presentations of two different analysts, David Tuckett describes this dual role of the presenter as a "curious situation":

> what they report about what their patients said and the interpretations they made are, in a manner of speaking, two versions of the same observation: the two authors have tried to report things as they believe they happened, but there is no getting away from the fact that the sense they made of what they were told must have operated to influence both their selection of what they attended to and reported and their interpretations. One might say that they both understand and construct: they participate in making history, and then report it.
> (Tuckett, 1993, p. 1180)

If clinical cases cannot function as a means of substantiating or supporting theoretical ideas or clinical practices, their role in what Klein called clarifying theories and ways of working seems much less problematic. Indeed, once freed from the burden of proving something, one might wonder whether clinical writing needs to be tied to a description of a real patient at all.

For instance, David Malan, in his textbook *Individual Psychotherapy and the Science of Psychodynamics*, uses an "imaginary therapy" to illustrate the main elements of psychodynamic practice. His rationale for this is that "no real example shows either clearly or completely enough all the features that I wish to illustrate" (Malan, 1979, p. 81), and so he elects to "make up an account of a fictitious therapy", based on the kinds of things that have occurred "in countless actual therapies throughout the world". This way of writing works by explaining to the reader what is going on in the analytic interaction.

This can be illustrated by looking at how this imaginary therapy begins. Malan sets the scene with the patient, a young man, telling the therapist, who is a trainee, that his problem is that he cannot maintain deep feelings in his relationships with girlfriends.

> The therapist sees that this inability to feel must represent a *defence*. She has ideas about what this is a defence against, but in accordance with the principle of exploring gradually and allowing the patient to do as much of the work as possible, she only gives a general interpretation: "I think this inability to feel (defence) happens because you are afraid (anxiety) of something that might occur between you and your girlfriend if you were to become more deeply involved"... This interpretation can be described as *asking a question of the patient's unconscious*... Without being fully aware of the significance of what he is saying, the patient now mentions that he had become more deeply involved with his first girlfriend than with the present one, but that she had not really wanted him, and when she had left him he had become very depressed and had spent long periods crying. After the break-up of a subsequent relationship, however, he had found himself consciously indifferent... The patient's unconscious has now in a sense exceeded expectations, since it has not only supplied the *anxiety*, but the *hidden feeling* as well.
>
> (Malan, 1979, p. 81, italics in original)

This way of writing situates the reader as an observer of a clinical encounter between patient and trainee therapist, while at the same time giving access to the teaching of the author, whose comments link the material to the relevant theoretical concepts and technical principles. It is similar to watching a tennis match between two players in the presence of a tennis coach, who is able to break down the particular strokes employed, as well as describing to you the game plan and strategy of each player. The account is given in the third person, as it is the teacher and not the therapist who directs the reader to what is relevant. We are given a small window into the therapist's subjectivity—"she had ideas about what this meant"—but her individuality is not developed but subordinated to her capacity to use theoretical ideas and follow principles of practice.

I think this clinical writing works, as it succeeds in demonstrating and explaining the concepts it aims to illustrate, while at the same time conveying the feel of a psychodynamic piece of work. Indeed, Malan makes a comment that many creative writers make about their work, that he had originally intended only to illustrate a few specific principles, "but the therapy then grew of its own accord" (Malan, 1979, p. 89). Malan also remarks: "I have found this piece of fiction extraordinarily easy to write, which has surprised me", which he thinks is because once the basic principles of psychoanalytic practice have been grasped "everything grows naturally and intelligibly" (p. 89).

I think the easiness in writing which Malan describes, as well as the success of this kind of writing, is a function of its generality, its applicability to a wide range of clinical situations. But this is also its limitation, the account of the interaction and process lack specificity, and in particular what it feels like to be this particular therapist with this specific patient. So this kind of account can serve as a teaching exemplar, a well-crafted illustration of general psychoanalytic principles, but it does not aim to be an exemplary description of real clinical work.

Clinical writing as a genre

If good clinical writing does not aim to substantiate or support theoretical ideas, nor to give a general account of them, what does it purport to do? Thomas Ogden, who has made a particular study of analytic writing, argues that it constitutes a "genre" of its own, one which involves "the conjunction of an interpretation and a work of art" (Ogden, 2005, p. 15). It is an "interpretation" as it organises and narrates the patient's life and experience in a particular psychoanalytic way so as to address "the relationship between conscious and unconscious experience". It is a work of art "as the writer must use language in an artful way if he is to create for the reader, in the experience of reading, a sense not only of the critical elements of an analytic experience that the writer has had with a patient, but also... what it felt like to be there in the experience" (pp. 15–16). So the characters, patient and analyst, who are the protagonists of this clinical writing "depend for their lives on the real people (the patient and the analyst); and bringing to life what happened between these people in the analytic setting depends on the vitality and three-dimensionality of the characters created in the story" (p. 16). But constructing these characters so as to render them vital and alive means that the clinical writer has to become "conscripted into the ranks of imaginative writers" (p. 16).

An important way of rendering the character of the analyst three-dimensional is to bring in the analyst's countertransference, that is, his or her "freely aroused emotional sensibility so as to follow the patient's emotional movements and unconscious phantasies" (Heimann, 1950, p. 81). A good example of how this can figure in clinical writing is given by Otto Kernberg, in a paper on working with "affect storms" in border-line patients. He gives a graphic description of his struggle to manage his feelings and retain his therapeutic balance with a severely acting out and provocative patient who drove him to his analytic limits. He recounts on one occasion growing so impatient with his patient's constant interruptions, misrepresentations, and refusal to listen to him that "in a strong voice, I told her she was talking sheer nonsense... I illustrated, point by point, in what way she had just distorted everything that I had just said, interrupting her as loudly as she would interrupt me while I was trying to say this" (Kernberg, 2003, p. 542). As soon as he had finished speaking, Kernberg described himself as having the shocking realisation that he had just "enacted the hateful, persecutory object that she had unconsciously projected into me".

> While I was thinking along these lines, the patient, to my great surprise, responded in a totally natural voice, and in a thoughtful way, that I couldn't tolerate her affect storms: wasn't the treatment geared to permit her to express herself freely in the hours? After a little while, recovering from my shock, I said: "I am impressed by the fact that you can only talk to me in a normal way if I talk to you as loudly and harshly as you talked to me before."
>
> (p. 542)

Kernberg utilises the concept of projective identification as communication (and so a version of countertransference) to understand what happened in this interchange, putting it down to the patient's ability to "register, for the first time in this session, my communication to her" (p. 543).

In giving such a vivid and honest account of his feelings and reactions, Kernberg creates a sense of immediacy and transparency for the reader. It is a mark of this quality that the reader can see things that might not be so obvious to the analyst/narrator. So Kernberg relies solely on the concept of projective identification, that he may have processed and detoxified the projections from the patient more than he realised so that she could take in what he said to her. But one can also wonder whether it was also his way of delivering his interpretation that had such an effect on his patient. For instance, his strategy of "interrupting her as loudly as she would interrupt me", which might seem to be disruptive of communication between them, could in fact be seen as a good example of what Daniel Stern has called "affect attunement", where the mother imitates her infant's gestures or speaking in such a way as to highlight certain affects (Stern, 1985, p. 138). This quality of the analyst/presenter supplying the listener or reader with more material than he or she intends is a feature of a good clinical presentation picked out by David Tuckett, in which "aspects of the investigation with his patient that are just about to become known and so permit the formulation of interpretation, may be preconsciously placed on a plate for the audience to see: the analyst knows but is not yet aware, as it were" (Tuckett, 1993, p. 1181).

This position that the analyst/narrator puts himself in, of his emotional sensibility being in advance of his more intellectual understanding, is powerfully conveyed in Kernberg's account in his description of his "surprise" and "shock" at the unexpected effect of his interpretation on the patient. This seems an example of the "curious situation" described by Tuckett in which the analyst/narrator is a participant in a history that he himself constructs. So Kernberg constitutes himself as a particular kind of narrator, one who writes as though he does not know what effect his interpretation will actually have on his patient—although this is, of course, a fiction because, as narrator, he knows precisely what is to come. This analytic sleight of hand, which is a commonplace of fiction but might seem to be problematic in assessing the value of a piece of clinical writing, is a feature of good clinical writing emphasised by Ogden:

> I find it is important not to know the shape of the story from the start, but to allow it to take form in the process of writing it. Not knowing the end of the story while at the beginning preserves for the writer as well as for the reader a sense of the utter unpredictability of every life experience: we never know what is going to happen before it happens.
>
> (Ogden, 2005, p. 18)

The importance of the beginning:
Freud's Rat Man case

This seemingly paradoxical position of "not knowing the shape of the story from the start" makes the way the analyst/narrator actually begins his or her account of particular importance: "the opening of a clinical account, when it works, has all the feel of the inevitable. It leads the reader to feel: how else would one begin to tell this story?" (Ogden, 2005, p. 17).

Furthermore, in choosing how to start, the analyst/writer makes an important statement about what he or she is trying to say:

> the place where one starts, in addition to providing an important structural element to the story and to the paper as a whole, makes a significant implicit statement about the writer's way of thinking, the sorts of things he notices and values, and, in particular, which of the infinite number of junctures in this human experience deserves pride of place in the telling of the story.
>
> (p. 17)

These remarks of Ogden's on how to open a clinical account provide a useful benchmark for looking further at those features that mark out a piece of clinical writing as being of high quality, and thereby capable of being thought of as an exemplar. I will look at two examples of how this has been done, one by Freud, whose case studies are prime examples of clinical exemplars, and one by a contemporary analyst.

Freud opens his case study of the Rat Man as follows:

> A youngish man of university education introduced himself to me with the statement that he had suffered from obsessions ever since his childhood, but with particular intensity for the last four years. The chief features of his disorder were *fears* that something might happen to two people of whom he was very fond—his father and a lady whom he admired. Besides this he was aware *of compulsive impulses*—such as an impulse, for instance, to cut his throat with a razor; and further he produced *prohibitions*, sometimes in connection with quite unimportant things. He had wasted years, he told me, in fighting against these ideas of his, and in this way had lost much ground in the course of his life. He had tried various treatments, but none had been of any use to him except a course of hydrotherapy at a sanatorium near—and this, he thought, had probably only been because he had made an acquaintance there which had led to regular sexual intercourse. Here he had no opportunities of the sort, and he seldom had intercourse and only at irregular intervals. He felt disgust at prostitutes. Altogether, he said, his sexual life had been stunted; masturbation had played only a small part in it, in his sixteenth or seventeenth year. His potency was normal; he had first had intercourse at the age of twenty-six.
>
> He gave me the impression of being a clear-headed and shrewd person. When I asked him what it was that made him lay such stress upon telling me about his sexual life, he replied that that was what he knew about my theories. Actually, however, he had read none of my writings, except that a short time before he had been turning over

the pages of one of my books and had come across the explanation of some curious verbal associations which had so much reminded him of *some* of his own "efforts of thought" in connection with his ideas that he had decided to put himself in my hands.

(Freud, 1910, pp. 157–158, italics in original)

At first sight, this might look like a medical case history. We are given an account of the Rat Man's main symptoms, their cost to his life, a history of previous treatments, and an account from the patient of his ideas on their origin in terms of his sexual development. It is also organised in a way not unlike Malan's imaginary therapy, in the clear way the different types of symptoms are described and differentiated from each other, promising a tie-up with theoretical ideas which are to come. But the "feel" of this introduction to the Rat Man case is quite different. It is more like we are witnessing a drama in which the workings of the Rat Man's mind, and the complex layering of his character, make their initial appearance in the context of this first instalment of the Rat Man's already developing relationship with Freud.

So the Rat Man's symptoms, as described by the Rat Man, are not simply listed or enumerated in Freud's narrative as in a medical diagnosis. In the opening of this introduction, they take centre stage, they become the italicised subjects of the account, their power over the Rat Man as seemingly independent forces over which he has no control conveyed in the cumulative effect of reading them one after the other, like the beating of a drum. Their effect on the Rat Man's life, the "wasted years", is emphasised by putting this phrase at the beginning of the sentence which follows the account of the symptoms—"he had wasted years, he told me", rather than putting the stress on the Rat Man's telling this to Freud.

This insistent stress on these impersonal forces which have come to dominate the Rat Man's personality and life goes hand in hand with a no less important emphasis on the Rat Man as a speaking subject. The very first sentence is about how the Rat Man "introduces" himself to Freud, and after telling Freud of his symptoms and the wasted years, the Rat Man goes on to offer Freud his own ideas on how his symptoms originated in his sexual development. This account portrays the Rat Man as an active seeker of sexual pleasure, though in a rather passive way. So the overall effect of this opening paragraph is to convey the battle going on in the Rat Man between these impersonal and powerful symptoms which dominate his life, and the thinking and speaking parts of his personality which are already organising the way he is speaking to Freud.

Then we get an account of Freud's first intervention, a question about the sexual origin of his symptoms. This question can look like the kind of question that might be asked in a medical examination. But it is actually a very different kind of question, not about the origin of his symptoms *per se* but about how the Rat Man *tells* Freud about their origin: why does he put such weight on sexuality? This simple question opens up an analytic space. It shows Freud to be interested not only in the Rat Man's symptoms but also, or perhaps primarily, in his character, that is, how he understands his symptoms and what kind of relationship he has with them.

The Rat Man's character is brought to light in the account of how he replies to Freud's question. Freud has already described him as both "clear-headed" and "shrewd". These characteristics have, I think, a rather ambiguous relationship to each other, "clear-headed" implying straightforwardness but "shrewdness" conveying a sense of the Rat Man only saying what he wants Freud to know. This is reinforced by Freud speaking directly to the reader to supply a corrected version of the Rat Man's answer—"actually, however, he had read none of my writings". Here, Freud draws on a well-accepted narrative device of drawing on knowledge of what can only have come later. He does this in order to present another side to the Rat Man's character, one in which he is an unreliable author of his own story (making the Rat Man a peculiarly modern kind of subject).

What has this opening narrative accomplished? In the opening sentence, the Rat Man had "introduced" himself to Freud by telling him of his symptoms. In the final sentence of this opening section, Freud tells us that the Rat Man had decided to "put himself in my hands". So in the course of this short opening section, we can see that the analysis is already underway and the outlines of the kind of relationship the Rat Man has started to develop with Freud established. We get a sense of the Rat Man's desperate willingness, indeed perhaps desire, to submit himself to Freud. But we also know that he has spent his life in submissive thrall to the obsessive/compulsive parts of his personality, and is now desperate to free himself from their power. This ambivalence around dependence and submission is evident in the confusion, comprised of doubt and vagueness, about how Freud's ideas have influenced him. Freud's narrative, both through its content but also its structure, shows this transference to be already in play, and prefigures its developing intensity as the case history unfolds.

A contemporary clinical account

Turning to a contemporary account of a clinical case, I have chosen one written by an American analyst called Ayesha Abbasi, published as part of the "Analyst at Work" section of the *International Journal of Psychoanalysis*, where the author's account of their work is sent to two other analysts, whose commentary is also published. I have chosen this example because, unusually, both commentators agree in describing this as a clinical account of high quality. The comments on the quality of her clinical work include her "excellent" use of the setting (De Posadas, 2012, p. 542), her capacity to function like "a carefully tuned instrument in the exercise of her analytic practice" (p. 537), and her "interpretive craft" (p. 542). Her writing is described as being narrated "in a spirit of great honesty" (Chabert, 2012, p. 539), resulting in "a document of exceptional quality, in the sense that the 'story' of the treatment is constructed and written in such a way as to transport us into the very scene of the analysis: this is due, presumably, to the magnetic pull of the transference in operation, as it is conveyed by the analyst's words" (Chabert, 2012, p. 545).

This is how Abbasi begins her account:

> I looked at my new patient, Mr. F. He was a man of medium height, with dark hair and eyes that were a startling blue. "My brother killed himself", he told me, sitting across from me in my office on a cold and dreary October afternoon. The words hung between us, heavy with what had not yet been felt or said by him. "With my gun. The gun he asked me to show him how to load and shoot with, a few days before he committed suicide. In the shower of the house we had been sharing here in town." I felt goose bumps on my arms and wondered if the thermostat in my office was set too low. I thought: "Fuck! Do I really have to deal with this?", and then, more soberly: "How will I ever help this man?" I said: "I am so sorry. What a loss for you—and for your family." Mr. F looked away, as though my brief words were like harsh sunlight in his eyes. I was struck by his inability to accept my words in some useful way and by his difficulty in expressing his own feelings about his brother's terrible and tragic suicide.
>
> (Abbasi, 2012, p. 515)

Unlike Freud's account, where Freud initiates the first analytic turn of the screw by his question to the Rat Man about how he is telling his story, here Abbasi's only reported comment is what sounds like a conventional expression of condolence. So it is not through her interventions but rather the way she describes her own mind and emotional sensibility, namely her countertransference, that we can see the opening up of an analytic space in her encounter with Mr. F. We see her moving from "Do I have to deal with this?"—a mark of something massively disturbing which she would rather not know about—to "how will I ever help this man?", now demonstrating some processing of her initial feelings and reactions in order to turn her attention to the clinical task in hand. We see her as an analyst in action when, after her "normal" expression of sorrow, she tracks what Mr. F does with this communication on her part, namely his inability to cope with her ordinary expression of sorrow and his inability to find his own words.

Although, in this opening paragraph, Abbasi's powerful and initially incapacitating reaction to Mr. F and his story of his brother's suicide seems to have been resolved, we are still left with her very first thought: "fuck!" In this opening paragraph, she does not comment on this, her thinking about the nature of this first thought only comes later ("an early warning about the very tight intertwining of love/sexuality and sadism in Mr F's mind"; pp. 517–518). The effect in the first paragraph of having this thought without any commentary conveys a sense of the analyst as both managing to master and process her strong reactions, and at the same time in danger of losing her analytic balance through the leaking out of reactions and parts of her personality that belong to her non-professional life.

The power of the gaze is another feature of the opening of this analytic case. Unusually for a clinical account, it begins with the first person: "I looked at my new patient…". This opening phrase frames this clinical case as a particular kind of engagement, a contest but also potentially an intimacy between them, the intensity of which might be too much for Mr. F to bear—"he looked away as if my brief words were like harsh sunlight in his eyes".

Perhaps the most striking feature of this clinical writing is the seemingly "novelist" aspects of the account. Why does Abbasi take care to report Mr. F's precise physical locating of his brother's suicide? Why make reference to what in most analytic accounts would be taken as irrelevant aspects of this first meeting, such as the weather or making reference to the thermostat in her office? The inclusion of her physical reactions, as manifestations of her countertransference, needs no justification, but these are also narrated in ways that seem banal if not bathetic: "goose bumps" on her arm, wondering whether the thermostat had been turned on too low. And why, in her account, does she choose as her opening remark to Mr. F an expression of condolence, which is not a normal way of opening an analysis? In my reading, these "ordinary" descriptions serve to set off the extraordinary way Mr. F begins the session, and can be seen as another rendering of the tension implicit in this paragraph between the professional and non-professional. Perhaps what is also conveyed is Abbasi's intimation that in order to keep her analytic balance, and perhaps sanity, with this patient she will need to anchor herself in her bodily reactions, the physicality of her office and the world outside, and the ordinary social conventions that bind people together.

Clinical writing and the analyst's subjectivity

According to Ogden, a mark of all good writing is that "the author disappears leaving traces"—"a writer learns in the course of becoming a writer how to get out of his own way and out of the reader's way"

(Ogden, 2005, p. 22). This is reminiscent of Freud's recommendations on analytic technique, that the analyst should keep his own personality out of the treatment (Freud, 1912, p. 118), for fear of influencing the patient through suggestion and thereby destroying the credibility and potency of the analytic process. As in his famous metaphor, "the doctor should be opaque to his patients and, like a mirror, should show them nothing but what is shown to him" (p. 118), good clinical writing seems to require a double effacement of the analyst's subjectivity, first as clinician and then as writer.

Certainly, what is conveyed in the examples in this chapter is the highly disciplined stance of the analyst, who reveals nothing of himself or herself except through the quality of attention to the patient and to the analytic work. This discipline can be seen as a putting into practice of what Freud calls the "opacity" of the analyst. The writing is also disciplined, all elements playing a part in the creation and evocation of an analytic experience, which is what Ogden appears to mean by the disappearance of the author: "good analytic writing is sparse and unassuming—just the essentials, not an extra word or repeated idea" (Ogden, 2005, p. 24).

Yet the examples of clinical writing I have given are full of the "traces" of the analyst, as both clinician and writer. Some of this, notably in the examples of Kernberg and Abbasi, is conveyed through the vivid and careful descriptions of their feelings and reactions to the patient and the analysis, what since Freud has been called countertransference. But although Freud had no analytic vocabulary to directly describe his feelings, what he felt about his patient and the effect on him of their first encounter can be traced through his way of writing. Indeed, what comes over most powerfully from all these examples is the presence of the analyst, as both participant and designer, clinician and narrator. This, I think, is the hallmark of good clinical writing.

All clinicians have struggled with the strictures laid down by Freud in the metaphor of the analyst being no more than a mirror, which seems to demand the obliteration of the analyst's subjectivity as designer of the analytic situation. The analyst's subjectivity has been partly brought back in again through the concept of countertransference. However, the kind of subjectivity licensed by this concept is only that deemed to have originated from the patient—countertransference literally means that which is "counter" to the patient's "transference". This leaves the analyst, as both practitioner and teacher, without a robust analytic vocabulary to write about the day-to-day "craft" of analytic practice, the kinds of ordinary skills needed to do the work. This is because to write in this way necessarily brings in the analyst's subjectivity as designer and constructor of the analytic process, the one who holds the mirror as well as being the mirror to the patient (Spurling, 2015). From this perspective, analytic writing can be seen as licensing another attempt to bring in the analyst's subjectivity, this time through the operation of the art and craft of the writing itself in conveying the experience of an analysis. In doing so, the author/analyst shows how they go about their clinical practice. For instance, the way Freud and Abbasi begin their clinical account shows a particular way of opening up an analytic space, as Kernberg's writing shows how he preserves or regains it. This is skilled practice conveyed with narrative skill. So good analytic writing can be seen not only to provide a more substantial and inspiring kind of "hearsay", but also a way for the analyst to narrate their own experience of becoming an analytic subject with their patient.

Chapter 7

The transformative other

Some thoughts on the psychodynamics of co-authorship

Ian S. Miller and Alistair D. Sweet

In this chapter, we focus specifically on some of those processes involved in collaborative thinking and writing, in an attempt to further explore and understand psychodynamic aspects of this approach to writing. Individually, we had both written and published extensively before meeting and before agreeing to collaborate on a number of writing projects. We were both also called upon, on a regular basis, to act as editorial reviewers for a number of high-beam journals, related both to psychoanalytic psychotherapy and psychoanalysis. It was in this latter capacity that we were informally introduced, when we were both asked to act as submission reviewers for the *International Forum of Psychoanalysis*.

Introduction (I. M.)

The present essay on the "writing couple" serves as a snapshot, an image in time. And like any snapshot, it depends on the technology, the contextual lens through which it is captured. I think of it as an old Polaroid image, destined to begin its fading the moment it is perceived.

In this, it is representative of an idea shared by us both, the development we recognise clinically and more broadly conceptually in the world of emerging psychoanalytic ideas, of a momentarily discernible expression we call "d" (Miller & Sweet, 2016; Sweet & Miller, 2016), itself a quotidian statement of the algorithmic clinical process long recognised in post-Kleinian thinking; and most prominently in W. R. Bion's elaboration of Melanie Klein's famous expression P/S<>D. Simply put, we have located a very regular occurrence between patient and analyst, in the daily work of psychotherapy: something every therapist knows but may not mark as significant.

Together, Alistair and I have shifted its theoretically capitalised, and so idealised, form. We have re-cognised it in a smaller-case font in recognition of our daily use of its articulations, continuously in play within the action of psychodynamic psychotherapy. And in parallel to the pairing of therapist and patient that is fundamental to the work of psychodynamic psychotherapy (Green, 1975; Ogden, 1994), our joint exercise in writing has pushed the boundaries of what each of us has articulated and thought individually, allowing another's thinking-through to try on the wild edges of thought, privately and confidentially—as in the space–time of a therapy session—as we wrest inchoate experience both central and peripheral within our clinical work into the domain of words and linguistic forms.

As I write, we are midway through the development of a book, building upon our joint essays; but importantly, headed into the complex and easily avoided knots of psychoanalytic thinking that individually might be averted—either by dissociative splitting or discrete repression and the turning toward other paths. Yet, together, our partnership, this productive assumptive group of "pairing", demands that we inquire together, each urging the other to deeper reckonings, because that is our task as psychodynamic clinicians.

Here, I suggest that the Bionian assumption of "pairing" is creative and productive, rather than an obstacle to the so-called "task" or job of discerning momentary psychodynamic truths. Bion's idea is a critical position both in his theory of groups and in his work with individuals. It is also a fundamental structural determinant of what we do as therapists: we meet our patients in a therapeutic pair or couple. Certainly, it is "sexual" in the broadest sense, that is, it is a sensual, felt experience. But it is also primarily epistemophilic in that it seeks to understand the world, along the lines of the hypotheses generated through the sexual theories of children (Freud, 1905d; Klein, 1932); and this productive push and pull of ideas, sometimes tender and sometimes blood-sport, is by turns comforting and aggressive. Homosexual? Perhaps. But more, as Daniel Boyarin (1997) puts it in assessment of the primary form of Talmudic study, itself a precursor form of the analytic pair, it is necessarily homo-social, a generative pair with the task not unlike André Green's desideratum for psychotherapy itself: the development through a detour in the other, of the self's generation of thinking (Boyarin, 1997; Green, 1975). Except unmistakably, together with individualised yields of thinking, there is pleasure in the company! Together, the diffuse and un-symbolised achieves mass and articulation, thick and often poorly spoken, before finding a space within the thinking couple, for incubation and confrontation with other, similarly percolating ideas.

Writing together is like our playing in the sandbox at an earlier age. Pure joy in the permission (as long as we "play nice") to build and destroy, to test the boundaries in saying what needs to be said and to accept (no matter how strange it sounds to the speaker in retrospective reflection) that the other will give it a fair hearing, beneath the blathered crudity of initial articulation. And then there are the moments of shared delight: in acknowledgement that one really has arrived, together with the other, in something substantive! Where else in psychoanalysis can one let slip a delighted war-whoop?

Part of the thrill of this discovery is in sharing the convergence of two individual journeys through psychotherapeutic trainings and practice across divergent (if broadly similar) careers. In this way, our arrival at the clinical articulation of "d" is itself what we now call (Miller & Sweet, 2018) an "emboldened d", in that it is a broader notion operating as a psychoanalytic landmark or marker, of theory: a concept traceable from multiple determining sources including: individual experiences in the conduct of psychotherapy; consideration of the developing ideas characterising the multiple stages of psychoanalysis (Green, 1975; Miller, 2016; Money-Kyrle, 1968); and the temporal holding or containment of long years of professional incubation as ideas shift and crumble, reconstituting themselves in the continuous leavening of clinical practice as we have come to know aspects of ourselves barely glimpsed decades earlier.

It would be incorrect not to credit, too, a shared psychodynamic value in observing the shift from the particularities of lived experience to the generalised universalities of ideas themselves recognised as "significant facts" within other particular arrays—the unique and complex skeins of experience brought to us by our patients.

Within this, we have discerned mutual respect for our respective journeys in self-development; and have recognised the hard-won achievement of such ego consolidation within the other. Yes, we have told each other our "foundational" stories; and without flinching. And have recognised the resilience that one comes to recognise in oneself, within one's partner: toward the consolidation of self among the fragments and fragmentations of multiple identities and historical experience. Northern Irish, Catholic, Protestant, secular, Jew, American, Irish, amid the Troubles, the Cold War and Vietnam, the Yom Kippur War, and 9/11, as well as the unique madness of originating families, traumatic sequelae to be worked through, and the quiet individual accomplishment of working through.

The specifics, of course, are personal. But the route through what has often been unspeakable toward the painfully contained and gradually integrated, until finally spoken between one to the other: that is shared and familiar to us. And our writing expresses such intuition in verbalised language, often referenced (perhaps too much at times) thickly with other clinical/theoretical/practical reflections through analytic history. We have travelled the same course and, now, focused on the analytic object of clinical practice, attempt to discern it beginning with eidetic imagery and ideogram through to verbalisation and consensual unpacking of the parataxic until we approach shared understanding. We have recognised too, having travelled very personal and particular paths, that sometimes such arrivals in consensus are merely transient platforms for future thinking—either dead-ended or productive.

How did our collaboration in writing come to be? From my side, I was motivated by a sense of estrangement and aloneness in a new, confusing place to which I had moved after a long career in a very different cultural setting; and recognised that there were too few individuals willing to risk the robust exchange of difficult psychoanalytic ideas. I have written about this elsewhere (Miller, 2015).

I remembered back to childhood and to a mother who would squawk in exasperation as I swam deeply immersed in a book, "go outside and play with the other kids!" Lifting my eyes, I looked at her incredulously. How was I to find kids, among the ball-players and skate-boarders, who cared about reading?

Half a century on, the same situation was before me, except that my mother was long gone and years of my own psychoanalysis had taught me a thing or two. I wanted to dig into ideas with someone willing to wrestle them into the ground (would that this were possible at my local pub, but this was psychoanalysis and not the GAA). And so I looked "abroad", across the northern border of the Republic, to Northern Ireland, less than two hours from Dublin by train.

First date

Not unlike a first date, the first actual meeting was full of overlapping, harmonious sounds and conceptual figuration. Each of us provided sufficiently good stuff, trustingly open stuff, so that it allowed the other to nibble happily at the edges. For me, the joy of meeting another kindred spirit in a field that is, at best, cautiously wary of difference and of betraying the darker side of clinical tradecraft, was thrilling. Not unlike a first date, or perhaps a chance meeting on an airplane, of strangers, speaking could be honest because there was no expectation of anything other than in the moment.

The facility of email allowed snippets of thought, generally agreed upon in direction, to begin to take place; and even if the directions we took were conceptually separate, the idea that the object we addressed was collectively affirmed was good enough. For me, at least, much of the exhilaration was in relief from the loneliness of composing thoughts where receptiveness might otherwise come only from editorial readers. Here and now, we shared the aliveness and tentativeness of play, with thinking-in-progress adding a dimension to the thinking-through of the privileged and dyadic work of psychotherapy.

Two general forms of composition occurred. The first was the writing, primarily by one of us, that was elaborated by the other; and the next was our recognition that the thoughts that were emerging from our partnership (however momentarily expressed by one or the other contributors) were deeply collaborative: that the transitory "product" of thinking could not have come to be without the interactive participation of the writing pair.

The first "trial" of this heady enthusiasm might well have led to disappointment, akin to the destruction of the clinical pairing resultant from the "negative therapeutic reaction" (Green, 1975; Riviere, 1936). What happened was simple: Alistair told me (when I was in the enthusiastic flush of ideas) that my ideas took us in the wrong direction.

Here, strongly felt, I experienced our difference; and it alerted me to the bubble of enthusiastic fusion in which I had been floating. First came a flush of sadness, that our paths had irreconcilably diverged (that is, the P/S fantasy was confronted with subjective realisation of D).

And with this, possibly anchored on the authentic togetherness I felt in our work, I experienced a sudden freedom. He was, after all, correct; but in a way unknown to him. His strong sense of our direction alerted me too, to my own unfreedom—a compulsive drift to continuing a single idea when so many other ideas beckoned. Writing itself had become automatic for me, a structure I had begun to follow, pulling the ideas beyond and forward rather than allowing the ideas to be stated and simply to "breathe" on their own. Did I want to write on compulsively as if the writing elaborated my earlier thinking, filling in gaps unnoticed earlier? Or rather, did I want to write (or not) on something else, something that had come at me obliquely, through our collaboration? In my identification with Alistair's position, I found myself freed from my own constriction!

This juncture established the importance of individual freedom in our nascent pairing. What was important is that each of us expresses in our own voice that which is important to us. And comments too, as when trying on a pair of new shoes, when the work, which is always new, feels like it chafes our psychic toes.

First contact and pairing (A. S.)

There is in the first contact with "another in the field" always, I think, a sense of curiosity, apprehension, and expectation. Actually it's only from this vantage point that I now appreciate how my initial contact with Ian provided an arena in which to situate and describe aspects of a concept we were later to work on together, namely transitions related to movements within the depressive position d/D (Sweet & Miller, 2016; Miller & Sweet, 2018). By this, we refer to the evolving capacities of both the therapist and the patient to more fully understand aspects of remembered experience, as this emerges, the ways in which patterns of behaviour continue to be replayed contemporaneously and how such patterns of relating are repeated in the therapeutic relationship.

Back then, however, that was some way off. We met by email, though I think it fair to say neither of us initially suspected how that particular form of communication would prove so central in the evolution and development of our collaboration as co-writers. For me, it was a marvellous opportunity to share with another tentative thoughts, ideas, doubts, and uncertainties connected to the vast fields of both theoretical and clinical psychoanalytic psychotherapy. Here though, I should add a caveat that relates to the apprehension I mentioned earlier. Having worked alone for a considerable number of years, the prospect of discussion, elaboration, and composition with Ian was both intensely exciting and somewhat daunting. Reflecting on my childhood experiences of, at times, both solitary reading and seeking out spaces to be alone in, where I could think, leads me to the realisation that my default position had been, until more recently, to work alone.

However, with Ian, I found a very willing co-collaborator and someone not in the least precious about his ideas. I also found a fellow traveller who was ever curious, questioning, and responsive to the ideas that came to my mind, often unbidden and in states of very early gestation. Coupled with this we were able to discover complementary areas of understanding and interest that had developed through the different training and work experiences we had undertaken. I soon found myself enjoying a discourse akin to locating an oasis in the most arid of deserts, having previously felt relatively isolated, as a researcher and writer. For me, one of the truly revelatory aspects of the creative relationship between us is the way in which so much of our joint work mirrors the actual mechanics of how we co-create. By this, I mean co-creative projection and introjection, operating much of the time either unconsciously or at a preconscious level. It seems to me that whilst one of us tends to be struggling with a particular idea or line of reasoning, the other, relatively unencumbered, often acts as a psychological receptor to accommodate, contain, and modify such ideas, before returning these now modified thoughts to the other. The parallel here to Bion's (1962) seminal paper on thinking is striking.

A web of thinking

Here's a recent example, which I hope is illustrative, of the way ideas may develop rapidly through the exchange of thoughts across emails. Nearing the end of a busy working week, during which I had a heavy schedule with both day patients and private evening appointments, Ian sent me an email on some ideas he had, related to the psychoanalytic defence mechanism splitting and the reversal of this. The brief exchange between us is reproduced *verbatim* and without alteration or addition:

I. M.: On this idea: the patient I mentioned just now, with the somatic conversions and translations, began at twice weekly; and in intensifying our work, through use of such translation, it has been necessary to increase sessions as a way both to metabolise "together", with a "witness", what is emerging (and to keep it safe) as well as to allow the already received "d" and reversal of retreat to "breathe", without particular emphasis in a given session on deepening awareness: that is, by allowing sessions themselves to have different rhythms and capabilities for holding in time. Here, I am underlining the "use" of the session as time-shared, tolerated in different qualities, by two individuals: ironically, the older, intensive psychodynamic format serves as a containment to tolerate understanding of the "good" self, capable of being thought.

A. S.: It occurred to me whilst thinking more deeply about this whole issue of the preservative retreat and reverse splitting that if the patient projects aspects of the fragile and needy self into the analyst, ostensibly as a holding function for safe keeping, this process in and of itself may provoke therapeutic impasse and drop out, precisely because the patient fears their own envious aggressivity now directed towards the fragile good object, so deposited in the analyst. The survival of one aspect of the self may now only be possible if distance from it is ensured, thus premature drop out from therapy. Ironically those analysts more skilled, in a receptive sense, of listening intently and receiving deep psychological communications from their patients may, paradoxically, promote distancing and therapeutic dropout with their patients, particularly if they move to time-limited, less regular (once/twice weekly) interventions.

I think it is worth noting the differences here, only perhaps possible to glimpse now at the vantage point afforded through hindsight and in the process of writing this chapter, of the surface and depth grammars (Wittgenstein, 2009) inherent within this communication, and in so doing moving from what is apparent at a communicative level to that which is largely unconscious and concealed.

The surface grammars ostensibly mark a discussion of dynamic processes conceived to be operating between analyst and patient. These include the notions of: tolerating different rhythms and temporal spacing, witnessing, projection of the fragile self into the analyst, as well as ideas related to psychic retreats (Steiner, 1993) and the reversal of splitting processes. Of course, at another level, the depth grammars also illuminate the hopes and fears of the writing pair, in close collaboration, during a phase when ideas are inchoate and emergent. To take a step back for a moment, from the personal context of the interchange; the pair become witnesses to each other, and are referencing in their own way each other's specific needs, wishes, hopes, fears, and anxieties, whilst mirroring the psychodynamics of the therapeutic pair.

Looking back on these rather *ad hoc* and fairly rapid email interchanges, of which I promise you there are many, I am reminded of musicians jamming together in the rehearsal room, before firming up ideas and taking them on to the stage or into the recording studio. In essence, I think this is what I personally find to be stimulating in our relationship as writing partners. And it is, perhaps, in this "potential space" (Winnicott, 2005) between writing partners that the primary elements of creative thinking are formed and emerge, leading to what might be termed the transitional idea, which then further propels collaborative work. The difficult part, I suppose, is remaining open to what may or may not emerge during times of need, and so tolerating waiting, as well as perhaps in a more perplexing way being prepared to live through considerable tracts of time marked by uncertainty and doubt. And of course, this is not at all unlike being in the midst of a therapeutic session, either as patient or therapist. Or indeed working through the totality of the writing process, which involves editorial review, copy editing, and proofing stages and so on, as necessary functions leading, eventually (it is hoped!), to the publication of one's work.

There is too something to be said about the ways in which difference can promote healthy debate and discussion leading to other ways of viewing and challenging many of the "sacred cows" which, perhaps for too long, have been given a privileged status within psychoanalysis. I joked with Ian recently during a lunch that though we had endured decades of bombings, shootings, and murderous atrocities in Northern Ireland, the majority of the local populous seem to find it practically impossible to complain in a restaurant! His retort: "For a Jewish New Yorker that's an art form!" This humorous quip perhaps goes to the very heart of many of the unconscious processes that ebb and flow between us, and no doubt other writing partners. Often one idea appears to be pregnant with another, whilst at the same time *relying on that which is other* to bring both ideas into existence. Central to this idea, of course, are processes of fusion and de-fusion, coming together—moving apart, negation, and creation.

Indeed, as our specific focus as co-collaborators has continued to evolve, sharpen, and develop, it is specifically with reference to both the generation of meaning and attempts to oppose it, negate it, and at times annihilate it that we have found ourselves increasingly concerned. Inherent in movements across the psychodynamic action landscape, both intra-psychically and inter-personally, and which we have denoted in our work by the lower-case d, we encounter fine-grained oscillations related to the process of change, that involve fusion and de-fusion phantasies, joining and parting, and the experience of fullness and emptiness.

These oscillations, developmentally in terms of pairing, may be thought of as initially rapid, or operating at "short wavelength", akin developmentally to pre-verbal primarily sensory relating. Given reasonably favourable conditions that promote the internalisation of a durable and robust containing object (Bion, 1962), the oscillations between the emergent self and its objects, including bodily part-objects, may slow and operate more regularly at "long wavelength". Another way to envisage this process, suggested to be evolving and unfolding across a continuum of d movements, is to conceive of a physical tension relative to forces acting upon one and another. Rapid oscillations at short wavelength suggest a greater degree of tension whilst a relaxation of this tension may be expected, as internalised containing capacities develop, perhaps leading to a greater sense of freedom and generative capacity, built on shared reflection and the capacity to appreciate the mind and the needs of the other.

So too in thinking together and writing together. As a creative pair, just as in the therapeutic relationship, there can be no substitute for the necessary admixture of ingredients needed to conjointly develop a secure base from which to venture further into, at times, unfamiliar and frightening terrains. Time and space and an appreciation of the other's particular use of these entities in the process of development, even if radically different from one's own, seems essential. If that is difficult at times, then so be it. The results are, in the end, very well worth it!

Chapter 8

The writer in the archives
Trauma, empathy, ambivalence

Phil Leask

A few years ago, one hot, dry summer—wonderful for swimming in the lakes or strolling by the river—I found myself in Berlin, busy with archival research. I was writing about humiliation during the years of the German Democratic Republic. I needed to find examples that would broaden my understanding of the nature of humiliation and the way it was used by a dictatorial regime. My favoured archive had eight thousand biographical items that "ordinary people" had deposited there, including letters, diaries, memoirs, and all the pieces of supporting evidence writers love to get their hands on: school notebooks and poetry albums; work diaries; formal deeds and documents proving birth and death, and finally wills.

My plan was to begin at the end of the war in Europe in May 1945. This was an end that was also a beginning, since Germany was suddenly divided into four zones of occupation that would evolve by 1949 into two separate nation states: West Germany (the Federal Republic of Germany) and East Germany (the German Democratic Republic or GDR). It was the period of transition I was interested in first. This was a time of chaos. In what would be the world's largest ever flow of refugees, millions were on the move, searching for a safe haven, while millions of others stayed put in the bombed-out cities, living in the ruins of what had been their homes. How, I wanted to read, did people manage to feed themselves, look after their children, avoid the prevailing violence, cope with their own suffering and loss, and accommodate the new authorities; and how did they feel about this? Having got that period out of the way, I would move on to the next, the forty problematic years of the GDR. The various divisions in time and space were clear; a set of historical ruptures marked out the breaks in people's lives, the moments when, because there was no other choice, everyone started over again.

But as psychotherapists know only too well, people's stories never start again so neatly from one day to the next. Whatever politicians might prefer to believe, there never is a "zero hour" when the slate is wiped clean, the horrors and crimes of yesterday are forgotten, and the old values abandoned, leaving only the future to be faced, whether with trepidation or hope. And so it was with the accounts I found myself reading: they began during the war and carried on beyond its end with no comforting sense of before and after. Where I might have looked to the writers for feelings of bewilderment, relief, guilt, shame, or horror, something that acknowledged what they, as individual Germans, had endured or done, or had seen others doing, or knew had been done in their name, only one thing was clear: life with its everyday imperatives went on, "Life with re- morseless forceps beckoning ...." as the Australian poet Kenneth Slessor expresses it.[1]

The historian is always looking for evidence, not the sort that would necessarily stand up in a court of law, but persuasive evidence, strong enough to justify his or her conclusions about people and the events they are involved in. (Is it not the same for the therapist?) In my case, looking for evidence of humiliation, I had to read long autographical accounts, memoirs, or batches of letters that extended over years or even decades. This reading of other people's writing took me deep into their life stories, stories that could be upsetting, not just to the protagonists but also, as it turned out, to me.

Let us consider one example.

During the war, the Kuhlmann family—Maria, her husband Joachim, and their children—lived in Rostock, a strategically important port and ship-building centre on the Baltic Sea. Their story comes largely out of let- ters written by Maria to her mother and sister in Hamburg.[2] At the time of the early letters, life for the Kuhlmann family was easy and comfortable; they had plenty of money, they went to concerts and the theatre and still had good holidays, even late in the war. Maria talks a lot about domestic matters, the children, toothaches and other minor ailments, and about enjoying life despite everything. Maria's husband, Joachim, was in a sen- ior position in the shipyards. He was often away on business and is a dis- tant but still important presence in the letters. Joachim was a convinced Nazi and it appears that Maria shared his views.

In early 1943, after the German defeat at Stalingrad, Maria expresses relief whenever she hears that someone in or connected to the family has not been on the Eastern Front. But in the end there is no escaping the Eastern Front: her brother, soon to be forty, is killed there in July 1944. As the bombing of Rostock intensifies, Maria and two of her children are evacuated to safety in a village south of the city. There they have one large room, one small room, and a cooker. The older children visit at the weekend; Joachim too when he is around.

By this time, a couple of days into the collection of letters, I am getting to know the family and feel myself involved, if not implicated, in their stories. Let me introduce you to Ludwig. At not quite eight years old, he is a particular delight: ceaselessly active, warm, curious, cheerful, and overjoyed to be living in this wonderful world. He appeals to me and I have, in a way, welcomed him into my life. Suddenly, he is caught up in a long and terrible struggle with some unspecified bowel disorder. He wrestles with it, and I can feel him suffering. Finally, there is no choice, he has to have an operation. This cannot be happening, I find myself thinking as I read on, fearful, anxious. Near the end of 1944, Maria writes that Ludwig—*my* Ludwig!—is "still drifting, unchanged, between life and death". He will not give in to his illness and has a second operation, but unless his wound heals, Maria says, "there is no longer any hope". Just before Christmas comes the fateful telegram from Joachim to Maria's mother: "Ludwig passed away". It is a shock: to me too. He was part of my life and now he has gone, just as I have got to know him, and I can do nothing about it. The fact that, as I read his story, he would already have been close to eighty, is neither here nor there. Maria's lament for her lost Ludwig is every parent's outpouring of grief at the death of a child, the impossible and inadmissable that nonetheless, despite everything, has happened. The pain is mine too, seventy years on.

What follows for Maria's family is often difficult and upsetting for them. They are required to have three refugees from the east in their tiny apartment. Maria on her own takes care of one of them, an elderly woman who was in bed for four months with a broken femur when suddenly she had to flee from the approaching Red Army. (Did she really have to flee? our authorities would be asking now. Was she really in danger? Was she not simply an economic migrant seeking a comfortable life in the West? Reading these stories, so many of them written by refugees, I cannot help hearing the current stories and the debates around them.)

Faced with the probability of a German defeat, Maria finds it hard to contemplate that all the gains made after the Nazis came to power and all the endurance of the population under the bombing could now prove to have been in vain. Joachim assures her that another fortnight is all that will be needed: presumably for Hitler's miracle weapons to have their effect. The letter is dated three days before Hitler's suicide.

In May 1945, following the Germans' unconditional surrender, Maria and her family try to make do in the "Russian Zone". Joachim keeps out of sight but is arrested at the end of 1945. The rest of the family flees to the West and endures terrible times in freezing camps with little food before finally settling in Hamburg. Joachim is released ten years later.

In passing, it should be noted that conditions in the British Zone, where Hamburg was located, were often no better after the war than in the Soviet Zone. Again the archives throw up painful accounts. Albrecht Bühler, looking back at his life—his family were also refugees—quotes from his mother's letter of January 1947:[3]

Albrecht is nothing but skin and bone, constantly cold and in a state. In Hamburg itself the awfulness of conditions is just too terrible. On the day before yesterday, on just one day, there were thirty suicides recorded. Here in Bergedorf two children froze to death and their parents hanged themselves. This extraordinary cold, and nothing to heat with and nothing to eat! How are we supposed to get warm? ... Two days ago I had to take Anita to the special babies' home, otherwise she too would have frozen to death on us.[4]

Anita was one of twins, born in July 1945. The other, Jens, died of malnutrition in September 1945.

Much is said these days about the importance of empathy, and much of it I agree with. Like so many examples dug out of the archives, however, the case of the Kuhlmann family highlights the contradictions and ambiguities around empathy. Sitting in the reading room in Berlin—well lit, warm and comfortable—I found myself looking in at myself, the writer at his laptop, patiently transcribing what he comes across, wondering how far he will get by the end of the day, thinking of lunch out in the square under the gaze of the scientist Robert Koch, the Berlin sparrows pecking around his feet, the nurses from the hospital nearby popping out for a quick cigarette ... And I saw and felt myself being moved by what I was reading, I felt the waves of sorrow, of empathy. Not just for Ludwig in his suffering but also for Maria and her other children and the elderly woman with her broken femur. (Of course the fact that I had fallen on a mountain in Germany and broken my femur in difficult circumstances six months previously may have had something to do with that.) These were people I had come to know, whose tribulations I had, in a way, shared. They were people like me. And yet they were a Nazi family. The children were too young to be blamed, and Joachim was too distant a figure for me to feel for, but I could see myself suffering with, empathising with Maria, whose social and political attitudes I found abhorrent and about whom I, as a historian, would want to write in cool, objective terms.

My point here is that empathy is not something absolute, something one has or does not have. Empathy can be selectively displayed and depends on the circumstances, not just on upbringing or personality or one's genetic make-up.[5] During the war, members of the SS showed as much empathy as one could wish to see—but only to one another; towards their "enemies" they showed none. It feels right to have suffered with and for Maria and Ludwig. It also feels right to reject Maria's political position and to acknowledge that in 1944, even as Ludwig was dying, I would, I hope, have been on the other side, seeking the defeat of all that she stood for. Equally, I do not feel I should show empathy towards Joachim—though that might change were I to go back and read his account of his time in one of the GDR's terrible prisons where acts of humiliation were a constant feature.

And so we return to humiliation ... Falling down a mountain is one thing; being pushed down a mountain is something altogether different. Both can be traumatic experiences, but trauma that is deliberately caused by someone else is far harder to come to terms with. This is where an act of humiliation, something always likely to be traumatic, is such a problem. I have argued elsewhere that humiliation is a demonstrative exercise of power that cannot be resisted, that it goes against all that was or could reasonably have been expected, lowers one's status or standing in the world, involves rejection or exclusion, and leads to a sense that an injustice has been perpetrated for which there is no remedy. The consequences are predictable and consistent and include, for instance, impotent rage and a desire for revenge.[6] It is the knowledge that an act of humiliation cannot, ever, be made not to have happened that is so hard to bear and the source of so much rage. Since there is no justification for acts of humiliation, whether in evolutionary terms or in terms of effective social interaction, it is my view that we have to empathise with the victim of humiliation and condemn the humiliator, *in any circumstances.* Even here, however, empathy is not absolute or indiscriminate. We can empathise with Joachim Kuhlmann if his treatment in prison involves humiliation, even as we abhor his actions as a Nazi. This is an important point for the GDR, and no doubt for any dictatorship. It can also be relevant to the therapist's individual patients who might, if we look closely, be both victims and perpetrators of humiliation.

In the GDR, a legal fiction declared that there were a number of independent political parties. In practice, it was the Communist Party—the Socialist Unity Party or SED—that was in full control and determined the actions of the other parties until late 1989. Internally, the SED was centrally controlled and the leadership had to be obeyed, all the way down the hierarchy to ordinary members. Humiliating errant members, and inculcating in its members the capacity to humiliate others, whether party members or ordinary people, was central to the way the SED exercised power.[7] This means that there are many times when we have to empathise with the ordinary party member who is the victim of humiliation, even if in other circumstances he or she might also be willing to be the humiliator.

An example of this too sprang from the archives in Berlin.

Joachim Goellner was a prisoner of war in the Soviet Union after 1945. In his much later autobiography, he talks of how he came to admire and love the ordinary Russian people, who were generous even in their own extreme poverty and the chaotic conditions caused by the German occupation.[8] Back in what became the GDR, he joined the SED. Some years later, he was appointed as a minor party official to promote cultural activities for the workers in the shipyards in Rostock. In 1961, he divorced his wife and married a younger woman whom he had made pregnant. For the SED, this was morally unacceptable behaviour by a party member and set a bad example to the rest of the population. Goellner was punished by being sent back to the shop floor to work in terrible conditions that caused him long-lasting physical damage. He was outraged by the injustice and hypocrisy of this, particularly as he could see higher-ranked party officials behaving in the same way without being punished. Nevertheless, Goellner kept his communist beliefs and stood by the party, until a second example of humiliation ten years later and then a third a few years after that. By this time, his life was falling apart and he showed many of the responses of someone who has been pushed down the mountain too many times: anger, depression, loss of empathy for others—even those close to him—and resorting to alcohol to overcome or hide from his feelings.

The hardest part to read in Goellner's account (which is supported by letters written at the time) concerns his children in the late 1980s. Two of his sons were arrested and imprisoned, one for theft, the other on what Goellner understood to be trumped-up charges. His third son tried to cross into Poland to reach the West German Embassy in Warsaw and so go to the West, but was arrested, imprisoned, and then expelled to the West. Goellner, sensing that his son was becoming desperately unhappy in Hamburg, made numerous requests to be allowed to visit him there. All of these were refused, even though Goellner was now over sixty, the age at which the GDR allowed people to make brief visits to the West. In 1987, his son committed suicide.

The postscript to this story is even more affecting. Goellner, driven mad by all that had happened, spent years writing obsessively to all in authority. He was desperate to turn things back to the way they ought to have been, wanting everything to have been different, wanting his son not to have killed himself, wanting the authorities to have allowed him to visit his son while he was alive, wanting the GDR not to have treated people the way it did. Only one letter received a personal reply. Goellner had discovered that his son was on a radio programme made by Norddeutscher Rundfunk. He wrote asking to be able to hear his son's voice, only to be told in an undated letter: "We are extremely sorry that we can no longer help you to hear your son's voice. The tape has long since been wiped."

One of the curious and difficult things about all cases of severe trauma, particularly those caused by the deliberate actions of others, is the way in which time stands still for the victims, even when they have apparently recovered and put what happened behind them.

For the victim, it is always as if the act of humiliation has only just happened. Consequently, the rage caused by humiliation is timeless: it always simmers just below the surface, waiting to be triggered. When, as in the case of Joachim Goellner, the traumatic events pile up one upon the other, there is in the end no relief: they are always present, the rage is triggered daily, hourly, dominating and destroying his life.

At this point, I find myself wondering yet again about the impact of such stories on myself. Am I too becoming obsessive, reading and thinking and writing about traumatic events, about humiliation, about suffering and endless rage? Almost nothing I find in the archives is as terrible as all the cases my colleagues have to deal with when re-searching the Holocaust. The second German dictatorship had shock-ing, unacceptable aspects but was nowhere near as bad as the Nazi dictatorship. But how does the writer, setting out to find evidence to support an argument, cope with such horrors, day after day, even when they are not as bad as those that appear elsewhere? What does it do to me to keep discovering people's largely forgotten stories, filed away in bomb-proof basements all around the country? They are all so individ-ual, these stories, so personal, so specific—as are the stories of people's lives presented day after day, year after year, to psychotherapists. Un-like the therapist, however, I cannot hope that over time things will change and that life will get better—or at least become bearable—for the people whose stories I am reading. It is too late; there is nothing to be done. I tell myself that these people, or their suffering relatives, have chosen to put their stories into the archives, hoping someone sometime will find them and be moved by them and write about them. Is their knowledge of that possibility therapeutic in itself? If so, I can perhaps comfort myself that what I am doing is a modest sacrifice in the inter-ests of improving the lot of people I write about, or of increasing other readers' understanding and therefore their appropriate sense of empa-thy. But all the time, day after day, I am bombarded by the rage that explodes from the written page.

Take Friedrich Kabelitz, for instance, whose account dates from the mid-1950s.[9] This is a story which provokes outrage from the start, and which we sense can only get worse.

On long winter evenings in the early 1950s, Kabelitz wrote down the story of his life. He was not intending to have it published; he simply wanted to record what had happened to him, perhaps to make sense of it to himself. However, the version in the archives is his second attempt at narrating his life, by which time he knew the dangers of writing some-thing that did not match SED's approach to politics, history, or liter-ature. While half way through his first version, he discussed it with a friend whose family he had helped. This friend passed the information on to the Ministry of State Security, the "Stasi". On 18 March 1955, the Stasi arrested Kabelitz and seized his manuscript. He was taken to court and on 27 July sentenced to four years' imprisonment. So much for friendship and loyalty, he notes.

Once out of prison, Kabelitz set about rewriting the manuscript. His story is full of contradictory and incomplete accounts, but is not self-indulgent or self-pitying. Fighting on the Eastern Front, he saw and apparently disapproved of terrible things the Germans were doing there. He writes vividly and approvingly of the Russian assassination of the *Gauleiter* (a high Nazi official and regional governor) in Minsk after his insistence on murdering the Jews there. A bomb in the Gauleiter's bed meant he "went flying up into the air and had to be scraped off the walls".

Kabelitz lost an eye and suffered a serious head wound early in the war. He spent much of the rest of the war not on active service but in logistics operations on the Eastern Front. For a while, after some mis-demeanour he does not discuss, he was assigned to a punishment battal-ion, laying mines and barbed-wire barriers and shoring up trenches and fortifications. This was, of course, extremely hazardous. Later, he was returned to an infantry battalion until a grenade ripped open his thigh. Somehow or other, as the German armies disintegrated, he made his way west ahead of the Red Army. Eventually he was taken prisoner by the Americans, put into an outdoor camp in terrible conditions, then trans-ferred, much to his disgust, to a French prisoner-of-war camp where con-ditions were even worse. Eventually released because of his injuries, he crossed illegally into the Soviet Occupation Zone to get to where he had lived near Magdeburg. He describes in detail the "Wild West" conditions at the time, and fighting off "bandits" who spoke Russian and were either Russian soldiers or, as he prefers to believe, Germans dressed as Russian soldiers. Having acquired some land and planted five thousand fruit trees on it as an investment, he worked happily enough in the new GDR, praising it and criticising it, and praising and criticising the Russians at the same time, as well as coming out with racist Nazi terminology about the "Asiatic hordes" from the east.

Kabelitz's story is long and often painful to read. He was constantly lied to and deceived by the GDR authorities and saw this happening to others around him. When he was sentenced for undermining the state, his house and land were confiscated. Later, he was offered them back if he would work for the Stasi. He considered this offer initially, but when they still failed to return his property, he fled to the West. Almost the only part of Kabelitz's account that moves away from unrelieved awful-ness comes from the West. There he shifted from a nationalist to a more internationalist way of seeing the world, though with strong Cold War elements. Some of what he says reassured me when I first read it; now it reminds me of our own losses as we in the UK—or at least, in much of England and Wales—turn our backs on the rest of Europe:

> All the peoples of Europe really should now, finally, set aside their petty disputes and end this business of time and again robbing one another of their best sons ... We don't need states any more. We don't even need national boundaries any more! We need Europe! A Europe that can not just feed its children but also protect them. Out of that we'll get the benefit of an economic standing in the world that will enable us all to do well. If that is not introduced, then we'll all go to the dogs. In any case, I thank my Creator that I had to go through the school of Bolshevism in order to understand this. Even at the price of losing my home and land and now having to start a new life.

So, a happy enough ending. However, there is a disturbing footnote to the Kabelitz story. He mentions in passing that he had a wife and young child in the early 1950s and that his wife was in hospital when he was arrested. There is no subsequent mention of her or of their child. The reader is left perplexed. Perhaps the way he had been treated—again, humiliated—left him able to focus only on himself, with no emotional space for them, no way of keeping them in mind. Or perhaps he was just a terrible husband and father. Or perhaps his wife joined in the denunciation and chose to abandon him, perhaps in order to get back the house and the land, a common enough story in the GDR. Too many "perhapses"! We can only speculate, something the historian wanting the truth out of the archives hates to accept.

Let us return to the GDR and its prisons. Several of the people whose stories I discovered spent time in prison. They write of their own experiences, but even more of the experiences of others whose sufferings they observe and find moving, disturbing or hardly believable.

In prison, the one-eyed Friedrich Kabelitz is an acute observer. After the horrors of his interrogation that lasted several months, with "methods from the middle ages that were used to humiliate and torture me", the prison he is sent to after his trial is a place of refuge and reassurance. However, we still see the vicious brutality of the warder known as "Red Annie" and hear the screams from the cell next door when she summons others to help her beat sense into a hostile prisoner. We hear this same prisoner being dragged down to the cellar where his screams are muffled and eventually die out. Then there are the Jehovah's Witnesses, banned for many years and constantly persecuted. They puzzle and fascinate Kabelitz, since they endured victimisation and torture under the Nazi dictatorship and are faced with the same under the communist dictatorship. What he describes is the one way people can refuse to be humiliated, through conscious, shared resistance. Such resistance involves the rejection of the values and beliefs of those with the power. Resisters refuse to accept that whatever is done to them will in any way break them or undermine their way of seeing themselves in the world. Ironically, this is how many of the communists imprisoned by the Nazis survived, by refusing to accept the authority and beliefs of those who could at any time do anything to them. The Nazi brutality, the communists believed, was only to be expected; it was part of what had to happen in the life-and-death struggle between the different classes that Nazism and communism represented. Sadly, the communists' way of treating their own prisoners reinforces the view that people who have been humiliated or brutalised by those attempting to humiliate them are themselves likely to resort to humiliation when in positions of power.

Another view of prison comes from Peter Erdmann's story and his Stasi file, both in the archives.[10] Erdmann was imprisoned for making and distributing leaflets expressing solidarity with Wolf Biermann, the poet and singer whose East German citizenship was revoked when he was performing in the West in 1976. Erdmann was badly treated before and after his trial and imprisonment, and only discovered after the end of the GDR in 1990 that he had been arrested because his ex-wife, with whom he was still living, had told the police about his actions. Definitely a case of being pushed down the mountain. Knowing nothing about that, he went back to live with her again after his release from prison.

Erdmann describes everyday brutality by the warders, as well as deliberate neglect, another form of humiliation. One of Erdmann's fellow prisoners suffered from a terrible attack of toothache. This was allowed to continue without treatment until the tooth was so rotten that it was finally removed. A more dramatic case involved a young man from one of the Asian republics of the Soviet Union who had deserted from the army while in the GDR and was caught trying to escape to the West. This young man was the son of a high Soviet official. On one occasion in the prison, he was pushed down a long flight of stairs by the warders and broke a number of bones. When he was about to be transported back to the Soviet Union before these injuries had healed, he tried unsuccessfully to commit suicide. Erdmann says: "Sadly—and I have to say this even as a Christian—this attempt failed. I would not like to know how he was then treated by our 'friends' [the common and politically acceptable description of the Soviet occupying forces]."

So much suffering, and so little time to absorb and process it.

In this particular archive, taking photos of the documents was strictly forbidden, so every day was a too-short day of reading and transcribing and trying not to think too much, beyond making connections and identifying useful points for the main argument. Our brains do not work like that, however. How many psychotherapists are able to hold themselves at arm's length from patients suddenly revealing terrible things that have happened to them, or that they have done to others? How many historians can keep their distance from the stories they are reading or hearing? We are moved, whether we want to be or not, by people's stories, just as readers of novels are moved by what happens to fictional characters. To cut ourselves off, to hold ourselves back, must display a lack of empathy, and without empathy, the work, the reading, the listening all become meaningless, if not harmful to those who are opening themselves up to us.

Yet again, the question of empathy becomes entangled with moral questions. How does one respond to suddenly hearing something truly shocking? A defence lawyer whose client declares, "I did it, it was me, I murdered him", is required to withdraw from the case and pass the client on to someone who is not allowed to know of this admission. The patient who admits to the psychotherapist to having done something terrible is still the patient the therapist has. Without empathy, is it possible to move forward? Is it possible even to consider how to respond to what the patient has said?

The academic world of literary "reception studies" is full of books and articles about how the reader—the implied reader, the imagined reader, the actual reader—responds to the written page, to complex and difficult characters, to cruelty, tragedy, loss and suffering. There is relatively little about the impact on the writer of the process of research—discovering, often when least expecting it, terrible stories—or of the subsequent writing up of the story. How do we get to grips with horror while holding the horror at bay? For me, as I sat in the archives, the Kuhlmanns, Kabelitzes, Goellners, Erdmanns, and so many others became my characters, my patients, my clients, even at times my friends. What happened to them affected me; what hurt them, hurt me; not as much, of course, but the trauma was transmitted as trauma can be, even if vicariously. I, the implied and actual reader, isolated and vulnerable, was left to deal with it, knowing there was no longer anything I could do for my adopted patients and friends. I read and I wrote and I listened and I felt. I suffered in silence or I talked of the stories endlessly; I dreamed about them or made up my own versions of them with happier endings; I presented them at conferences, wrestled with them in articles, wrote book chapters about them.

Empathy, trauma, ambivalence: the abstract concepts and the reality of peoples' lives reach out from the written page, swirling around me, restlessly and obstinately bringing forth yet more written pages that in turn yearn for yet more imagined readers: a virtuous circle, one can only hope, that makes us think and feel and write, and write and feel and think, and then settle down to write some more.

Notes

1 Kenneth Slessor, "Sleep", in *Poems by Kenneth Slessor* (1957).
2 6779 Kuhlmann family letters between Rostock area and Hamburg, 1939–1946. Kempowski Biografienarchiv, Akademie der Künste, Berlin [henceforth K Bio] 6779. To protect the families concerned, the names here and in other examples are pseudonyms.
3 The translations from the German are my own.
4 Albrecht Bühler, Beiträge zur Familengeschichte der B. im 20. Jahrhundert. K Bio 6894.
5 Here I disagree with Simon Baron-Cohen, who does not look at people who can display both empathy and a lack of empathy, according to the immediate circumstances: Simon Baron-Cohen, *Zero Degrees of Empathy. A New Theory of Human Cruelty* (2011).
6 Phil Leask (2013), Losing trust in the world: humiliation and its consequences, in *Psychodynamic Practice, 19(2)*: 129–142.
7 Phil Leask, Humiliation as a weapon within the Party: fictional and personal accounts, in M. Fulbrook & A. I. Port (Eds.), *Becoming East German: Socialist Structures and Sensibilities after Hitler* (2013).
8 Joachim Goellner, *Autobiographie Die wundersame Reise des Odysseus des XX. Jahrhunderts*, K Bio 6860/1.
9 7043 Friedrich Kabelitz, *Lebenserinnerungen Friedrich K., 1939–1956*, Kbio 7043.
10 Peter Erdmann, *Stasi Files and related Procedural Files*, K Bio 6232.

Chapter 9

An I for an I
The construction of a written self

Cheryl Moskowitz

In first-person writing, just as in psychoanalysis, the subject tries to construct a narrative that comes as close as possible to matching who they think they are or would like to be. But this may prove an impossible task, and a risky one. What we risk when we enter analysis, or set out as a writer to write about ourselves, is loss. We risk losing what we thought we knew as absolute and true. We let go of fixed identity or any sense of certainty about ourselves and enter instead a hall of mirrors in which every way we turn reveals new possibilities and perspectives.

I'm interested in what happens to the "I" who is telling the story, in both these processes. Particularly when the patient or writer reaches a point where certain aspects of their story become impossible to tell. Impossible perhaps because there are things they simply can't remember well enough to give an accurate version, or because there are elements that feel too painful, too exposing, too uncomfortable to reveal to the analyst or on the page. Either way, there will be a gap, a circumvention in the telling. In selectively telling the story of who we are, do we risk losing the part of ourselves that we are not able to tell?

Christopher Bollas says:

> First, when we think "me" without reference to any other term, we evoke a dense inner constellation, a psychic texture, existing not in the imaginary, although it yields derivatives there, but in the real, an area that can be experienced but cannot be represented in itself.... writing about such a mental phenomenon is not only hazardous but based on the false premise that the elusive "me as real" can be written about.
>
> (1997, p. 152)

Adam Philips suggests: "Psychoanalysis as theory and therapy, can never be useful—despite Freud's commitment to the progressivism of Science—as a way of putting us closer to the Truth" (1994, p. 67).

Certainly, it is common for anyone telling stories about their past, particularly those concerning very early childhood, to come to a point when they are unable to tell any more what is true and what is not. Even in AD 400, St Augustine confessed, "This period of my life, which I cannot remember having lived, which I take on the word of others, and which, no matter how reliable the evidence may be, is still a matter of conjecture..." (St Augustine, in Bruss, 1976, pp. 1–2).

The reciting of particular memories, especially those that are often repeated, can feel rehearsed, and the process of remembering soon becomes more anecdote than recall. Unless one is simply setting out to supply the facts, specific dates or times and so on, about certain events, and has supporting evidence to do so, most stories we tell about ourselves must be taken at face value without verifiable proof. In this situation, for the teller, truth becomes interchangeable with invention. However veracious the subject might want to believe themselves to be when talking about their past, they find themselves confined, as St Augustine did, to conjecture. "When, nowadays, I attempt to follow in memory the winding paths from one given point to another I notice with alarm that there are many gaps..." (Nabokov, 1967, pp. 101–102).

The whole process of telling one's story can begin to feel like a confabulation, an attempt to plaster over cracks and fill in the holes. Nothing remains certain. "One shouldn't write one autobiography", the French psychoanalyst, J.-B. Pontalis wrote, "but ten of them, or a hundred because, while we have only one life we have innumerable ways of recounting that life to ourselves" (Pontalis, in Philips, 1994, p. 73).

According to Freud, however, we shouldn't do it at all. "What makes all autobiographies worthless", he writes in a letter addressed to his nephew, Edward, in 1929 "is their mendacity". An American publisher had just made an offer hoping to entice the great man to write his own, but Freud staunchly maintained that there were only two conditions under which biography, or indeed autobiography, could be justified: if the subject has had a share in important, generally interesting events; or as a psychological study. However, he explained in correspondence with his nephew, even if one or both conditions were met, to write a psychologically complete and honest confession of life would require so much indiscretion about those who might still be alive "that it is simply out of the question" (Freud, in Mendelsohn, 2010, p. 68).

In her seminal book *Becoming a Writer*, Dorothea Brande insists, "the first step toward being a writer is to hitch your unconscious mind to your writing arm" (Brande, 1996, p. 63). Brande's book sheds light on the writing process but, more importantly, on what it is to *be* a writer. Though first published in 1934, the book contains insights which, to my mind, have never been bettered on the subject. The book was written in Freudian times and Brande understood writing to be, as Malcolm

Bradbury put it in his foreword to the 1996 edition of the book, "essentially a psychological matter: at once a conscious activity and an unconscious one". Reconciling and balancing the two "is an essential part not just of the process of writing, but becoming a writer in the first place" (Bradbury, in Brande, 1996, p. 13).

But perhaps there is a price to pay to achieve this balance. When titling this chapter, I had in mind something to do with exchange. I was interested in exploring not only the difficulties, risks, and sacrifices involved in writing the self but also what gets traded for truth in this process and what might be gained from such a trade-off. The "eye for eye, tooth for tooth" saying from the Old Testament tells us that punishment should always be equal to the crime or offence or, put more simply, that a life must be given for a life taken. Applying this to first-person writing could imply that in creating the literary "I" on the page—a necessarily inventive process—the writer's true self is sacrificed, subsumed by the fictional version of themselves they have constructed in their autobiographical narrative. The "lie" becomes the new "I".

I believe we are all, as human beings, concerned with preservation of self and that all human endeavour, however else it might be judged, can be understood in terms of this single objective. A threat to our person is also a threat to our sense of self-worth and vice versa. That is not to say we are always successful in our efforts to avoid such threats. "People come for psychoanalysis when there is something they cannot forget, something they cannot stop telling themselves about their lives", says Adam Philips.

> And these dismaying repetitions—this unconscious limiting or coercion of the repertoire of lives and life-stories—create the illusion of time having stopped. In our repetitions we seem to be staying away from the future, keeping it at bay. What are called symptoms are these (failed) attempts at closure, at calling a halt to something. Like provisional deaths, they are spurious forms of mastery.
>
> (Phillips, 1994, pp. 13–14)

It is, of course, that same inability to forget that drives the writer to commit certain stories about themselves to paper, imagining perhaps that if they can do this successfully once and for all, it might allow them to move on, beyond themselves, to other subjects with less fixed narratives promising new imaginative possibilities. Even the impulse to keep a journal, it seems to me, is the writer's attempt to rid themselves of the burden of constant repetition. But, in trying to know ourselves and set that knowing down in an absolute way or articulate something too immediate or close to the bone to be put into words, we lose sight of what we thought we knew and are left with only a compromised sense of ourselves.

But might there be another way? Borrowing from psychoanalysis, might it be possible to find a new way of knowing through the stuff of dreams and the imagination, to let the unconscious be the driving force and thereby gain an increased sense of self and further self-knowledge? Throughout her book, Dorothea Brande stresses ways that "the writer (like every artist) is a dual personality". "It is the writer's intellect", she claims, that "directs, criticizes and discriminates wherever two possible courses present themselves, in such a way as to leave the more sensitive element of [his] nature free to bring forth its best fruit" (Brande, 1996, p. 139).

Here, Brande could almost be talking about the role of the *ego* and the *id* and the way the former must be caretaker of the latter and how each aspect of the writer's personality must learn to make way for the other at different points of the writing process. None of Freud's writings are specifically mentioned amongst the sources Brande lists in her appended 1934 bibliography, but there is no doubt that she was influenced by certain Freudian concepts and in dialogue with them. In some ways, *Becoming a Writer* could be read as both a response and a rebuttal to Freud's 1908 paper "Creative Writers and Day-Dreaming".

Freud, in this paper, portrays the writer as an essentially dissatisfied or unhappy being—albeit a fascinating one—and emphasises the role that day-dreaming and, in particular, "phantasying" born out of unfulfilled wishes, has to play in the writing process. Freud insists on the importance of the "unreality of the writer's imaginative world" for the technique of the art and suggests that the writer "creates a world of phantasy which he takes very seriously—that is, which he invests with large amounts of emotion—while separating it sharply from reality" (Freud, in Gay, 1995, p. 421).

Freud sets out his paper with the disarmingly passionate *cri de cœur:*

> We laymen have always been intensely curious to know—like the Cardinal who put a similar question to Ariosto—from what sources that strange being, the creative writer, draws his material, and how he manages to make such an impression on us with it and to arouse in us emotions of which, perhaps, we had not even thought ourselves capable.
>
> (Freud, in Gay, 1995, p. 420)

Brande, on the other hand, whilst paying important tribute to the elements of "genius" and "magic" involved in the work of a writer, seeks early on in her treatise to emphasise that writing is a healthy combination of will and imagination, hard work and determination, and a capacity to give way and be responsive to unconscious processes whilst possessing the awareness and skills to rein them in when necessary. Brande is concerned to dispel held myths, such as the picture of the artist as "a monster made up of one part vain child, one part suffering martyr, and one part *boulevardier* [fashionable socialite]", and sets out instead to remove pathological associations from, and demystify as much as she is able, the processes involved in "becoming" a writer (Brande, 1996, p. 35).

Freud regards creative writing to be at once a mysterious process and a symptomatic one indicating the writer's need to escape and separate from what is real, whilst Brande insists more pragmatically on writing as a discipline that demands a high level of self-awareness and must be determinedly practised, learned, and discovered in order for the real magic to occur. I would argue for a third definition, combining both perspectives which could relate especially to the task of writing oneself, as authentically as possible, in first-person autobiographical writing.

Psychoanalysis, Malcolm Bowie writes, "is overwhelmingly concerned with the production and transformation of meaning. Whatever cannot be transformed, psychically processed, reiterates itself. A trauma is whatever there is in a person's experience that resists useful redescription. There is no future in repetition" (Bowie, in Phillips, 1994, pp. 13–14).

The task, for the autobiographical writer, is to find a means, through reinvention, of coming closer to the truth. Writing about oneself may always require one to lie—the art is to find a way to tell those lies honestly.

Nearly twenty years ago, I set out to write my own life story, which was published as the novel *Wyoming Trail* (1998). *Wyoming Trail* deals with autobiographical material and is written in the first person. However, when discussing with my publisher where to "place it on the shelf" we agreed to classify it as a novel rather than a memoir. Though I believe the material in my novel to be honestly and truthfully told, it did not feel accurate to define it as non-fiction.

Bollas says, "It is interesting that we do not have such a precise inner experience of our own self as we do of an other, but surely it is because 'we' or 'I' is too near to experience to become its own signifier: it cannot call itself into delimited representation" (Bollas, 1997, pp. 148–149). The tools of fiction can serve to liberate and minimise some of those delimitations. Simple techniques like renaming can create distance, provide a protective mask for the "I", and cloak it with enough invention to allow us to see ourselves afresh, as if we were the other.

In *Wyoming Trail*, I named the main character (me) Francine. And I gave new names to the family members: my mother became Alma, my father Leon, and my two sisters Cynthia and Melanie. Consciously no doubt this was in part a courtesy, an effort to protect the identity of those who were bound to feature in my writing. But in retrospect, I can see also that there may have been a more unconscious motive driven by an instinct to get closer to the truth, not further away from it. By assuming the right and the responsibility to rename those who already had names, I was doing what an adoptive parent might with a child they have decided to commit to, or what we might all have done as children ourselves to mark possession of a special doll, pet, or toy. I was making them my own, owning my relationship with them, and in the process revealing much more about the "I" that was doing the choosing than those who were having new names chosen for them. I was endowing them with my own associations. I was preserving a part of me—that is my specific personal relationship to each one of them—rather than to risk losing it (as I might have done had I used their real names) to the more amorphous sphere of public identity.

I wrote the book in three parts. The first part establishes the land-scape of my childhood, western United States, which is also my inner landscape as a writer, and this part ends by having to leave that place, aged eleven, to begin a new life in England. This was my America, told through the eye, through the "I", of Francine. The remembering in this part is a bringing together of the parts of my early experience that floated to the top; recurrent dreams, parents arguing, visits with Grandma, the birth of my younger sister, and eventually, arriving as a stranger in a strange land.

Initially, when setting out to write the book, one of the main questions I wanted to pursue was the effect of dislocation on identity. I was aware of having to discover ways early on to adapt to sudden uncertainty and change. The need to exercise control over myself and those around me became a key issue for me growing up, manifesting most significantly as anorexia, from which I suffered as a teenager and into my early adulthood.

Around the time of writing *Wyoming Trail*, I read Eva Hoffman's *Lost in Translation*, the story of her family's move from Poland to Canada in the late 1950s. Though her story of emigration contained many elements that were different to my own, I strongly identified with many of her observations and was drawn by the telling of her experience. I wanted, as a writer, to be able to achieve a similar accuracy of emotional detail in terms of what it had been like for me to move with my family from America to England.

"Loss", Hoffman writes, "is a magical preservative. Time stops at the point of severance, and no subsequent impressions muddy the picture you have in mind. The house, the garden, the country you have lost re-main forever as you remember them" (Hoffman, 1989, p. 115). I hoped that this might hold true for me in my writing, although I also feared that the opposite might happen. By daring to write about what I had left behind, I worried I might be in danger of losing it further.

Amongst the questions Hoffman asks in her book is, what happens to language when a person changes country? Though I was not switching languages, I identified with Hoffman's sense of foreignness and the need to establish new definitions of things.

I am not a plot-driven writer. I am propelled instead by questions. So, even though I knew the story I was telling was my own, I did not know exactly what would happen or where the story would take me. I was driven primarily by the question of identity. How (not why) do we become who we become? And I suppose the sub-question, if there was one, was "can we be defined as much by what we imagine as what we know?"

The second part of *Wyoming Trail* explores adolescence and young adulthood and traverses between the real and imagined. The "I" in the piece, the me, Francine, journeys to find her father Leon who has estranged himself from all family members. She finds him lodging first with a pair of female mountain climbers in a lesbian relationship, and later in a mansion where he is being "sugar-daddied" by a millionaire homosexual art-dealer whose wife, by convenience, is dying of cancer. None of these details needed to be invented, lending veracity to the saying *truth is stranger than fiction*. Certainly, I was finding that the honest telling of my story contained such an abundance of sensational material that it was often hard to quell the scorn of the inner critic—surely you must be exaggerating! But I was not—indeed, in my quest to hold on to a real sense of a past I genuinely feared losing, exaggeration would have served no purpose.

I know, from my position as a therapist and from being in analysis myself, that it is common for a patient to feel embarrassment or shame about the material they are bringing, but also the need to insist to the therapist that they are not making it up. It is feared that the more shocking or lurid details might be, the more they will be assumed to be exaggerated. However, even if the therapist does not baulk at such detail, the patient worries about it being "too much". Maybe all our telling of the past is like that, our remembering of it having caused it to concertina into a tight wadge of overwhelming intensity. In his book *On Flirtation*, psychoanalyst Adam Phillips writes, "People come for psychoanalysis when there is something they cannot forget, something they cannot stop telling themselves..." (Phillips, 1994, p. 22).

Once I had dealt with the child and young adult parts of my life in Parts One and Two of *Wyoming Trail*, I felt somehow that the only thing to do would be to bring the story up to date and write about my life in the present. Reluctantly, I began to write a Part Three with this intention. I say reluctantly because it seemed to me that there would be no way to find anything to say that would not come across as extremely reserved or stultifyingly dull about the present. Imagine being told that you must keep your bedroom curtains open at all times for whoever wants to look in. You would, quite simply, no longer act naturally, whatever is on show would only be revealed in a self-conscious, carefully monitored, and censored way. That may be compelling enough for a staged reality TV programme like *Big Brother*, or an art exhibition where time is deliberately slowed (like watching Tilda Swinton asleep for hours inside a glass box as part of Cornelia Parker's 1995 *The Maybe*), but my intention with the writing was to use it as a process, to understand something more about myself. To attempt to answer the question "How do we become who we become?", not simply to bare all just for the sake of it.

The third part was not right and I began to lose heart with the project altogether. I had not set out to simply report on my life and bring it up to date, I had not risked losing myself in the telling to disappear under a veil of banality. Not only did I feel like abandoning what I had done already but I wanted to destroy it. I thought, dramatically, of throwing it on the fire, like Robert Louis Stevenson did with his first draft of *Jekyll and Hyde*. In Part Two of *Wyoming Trail*, my anorexic alter-ego Francine burns pages from her diary and scraps of paper on which she has written vows to herself. She burns them and rubs her face in the ashes. And for what? To claim back or to expurgate?

I felt suddenly that I was playing a very dangerous game, and in trying to establish a sense of who I was, and who I am now, through writing, I was instead being pushed so far off balance I no longer had a sure footing. It is not an accident that so many first-person memoirs are written by those who have been uprooted from place, from culture, from family, health, or whatever is familiar. The effect of dislocation is disintegration and writing can be a way of trying to re-integrate. To connect with a past you have left behind, and perhaps make sense of the present that you now find yourself in. But "Things fall apart; the centre cannot hold", as the third line of Yeats' 1919 poem "The Second Coming" tells us. Far from working to integrate my past and present selves, I was afraid that my attempts to write about any aspect of myself would undo me even further.

We came to England from America with suitcases, nothing more. My home, my friends, my toys, my American identity all left behind. Then my father left too, without a trace. Up until the writing of *Wyoming Trail*, I had tried to keep those things alive—my America, my father, my home—in my head. "Nostalgia is a source of poetry, and a form of fidelity. It is also a species of melancholia, which used to be thought of as an illness…" (Hoffman, 1989, p. 115). Now I had given them away, and I felt myself to be in danger of falling into a void with nothing to hold on to and no stories left to tell.

In psychoanalysis this falling apart, this place of nothingness, this arrival at a cliff edge facing an empty void, could be a marker of success—an indication that the analysis is proceeding as it should be, that patient and analyst are both properly *in* the process; that the thicket of endlessly repeated material has finally been got through, a clearing. The way is clear for moving on, stepping off that cliff edge together, into the void of the new.

I had been in once-a-week psychotherapy for a couple of years before beginning *Wyoming Trail*. During that period of therapy, I'd been working on my first piece of long fiction, *The Only Sound There Ever Was*, a novella that remains unpublished, written from the point of view of a therapist who gives up all her patients in order to spend time exclusively with only one; a girl who arrives on her doorstep blind, deaf, and unable to speak. It is not hard to see what I might have been wanting to explore in that first fictive narrative. *Wyoming Trail* was different, I was not making up a story, I was writing *my* story, and by the time I'd reached my point of stuckness with Part Three, I'd left my first therapist and entered into five-times-a-week psychoanalysis.

By now, a literary agent had taken an interest in me and my unfinished novel, yet I was still ready to throw everything in the bin. "What are you afraid of?" my husband asked me. I knew the answer to his question immediately. I'm afraid of losing my memory, I told him. My memories were all I felt I had left of my place of origin, my original self. I was afraid that having written everything I could remember about my past I would now no longer be able to retrieve any of it. I was afraid of forgetting and losing my ability to remember. Then you have to write that, my husband said.

I have often advised those I care about—my children, friends, family, those I work with—that a good way to deal with the anxiety or fear of something happening is to "travel" down the road of the imagination as far as you are able, imagining that the thing you are anxious or worrying about is actually happening, in order to understand that fear better and to find a strategy that might help to confront it. My husband was right—it was time for me to apply the same thinking to myself and dare to dream the worst.

Dreaming was considered by Freud to be the "royal road to the unconscious", and I was very aware, as a patient, of how pleased and excited my analyst became when I brought details from my dreams into the analysis. In the beginning, this had perplexed me. A dream is, after all, made-up material. Pure invention, albeit of the unconscious mind. But nonetheless this stuff of invention presents as gold dust to the analyst. There is a strange kind of moralistic imperative involved for the patient bringing a dream into analysis. What is to stop the patient lying about a dream they have had, using their conscious mind to make up a fantastically interesting dream they can then tell in analysis? The telling of a dream must be honest or there is surely no value in it. But the excitement of the analyst in receiving the dreams of the patient encourages more dreaming. The patient *wants* to dream for the analyst (whether consciously or unconsciously). And whatever the patient is capable of imagining enables the analyst to also imagine, on the patient's behalf. Finally, it becomes clear, that whatever truths are being looked for will be found in the space between these two imaginations.

I began to write Part Three. Fuelled by my fear of forgetting, I imagined myself into a state of being, some way into the future, at an age I had not yet reached and at a stage of life I had not yet experienced.

The narrator "I" has lost the ability to remember and can no longer recall the parts of her life that have gone before, and therefore has new attachments, to people as yet unknown, and experiences not yet had. These attachments and experiences are, nonetheless, quintessentially a part of who I, my character Francine, is.

The psychoanalyst Christopher Bollas suggests that the future—future selves and states of mind—arise through a process of evocation. That is, by imagining, by consciously constructing our dreams we can bring certain parts of our selves to life. "To be a character", writes Bollas in his book on that subject, "to release one's idiom into lived experience requires a certain risk, as the subject will not know his outcome; indeed, to be a character is to be released into being" (2014, p. 54).

During the course of the Creative Writing and Personal Development MA at Sussex University, on which I taught from 1996 to 2010, I developed a writing exercise for the students to encourage them to imagine their own future selves. I asked the students to try what I'd had to do to regain a sense of myself in my own narrative in *Wyoming Trail*: Think of a time some way ahead of where you are now. Place yourself somewhere you can imagine yourself being in that time and then imagine someone who you have not yet met, but who, in this future time and place, has become a significant figure in your life. Write yourself in relation to that other.

In psychoanalytic terms, the individual knows of its existence primarily in relation to the other. We know that we exist, that we are real, because of the way we experience ourselves as reflected in the eyes of someone else. As the French psychoanalyst and philosopher Jean Laplanche says, "The other person is primal in relation to the construction of human subjectivity" (Laplanche, in Laplanche & Fletcher, 1999, p. 260). There would be no first-person writing without the other person to read it.

In the end, I believe the self must be defined by the capacity of the imagination, as well as the real lived experiences of the individual. What we lose in remembering we gain by imagining. In human terms, the remembered self and the imagined self are equally flawed and equally true. An I for an I, then, is neither punishment by sacrifice, nor replacement by exchange, but a fundamental part of constructing and gaining a written self.

Chapter 10

Configuring words

Joan Raphael-Leff

How does one write about writing?

This is the most difficult writing task I have ever undertaken. If expressing my own voice in writing is one way of authorising a sense of "generative agency", investigating it is a daunting task, necessitating self-consciously peeling back the layers to render an unconscious process of gestation visible.

Writing's origin is mysterious. Even as vivid a writer as Freud pondered how a "dreamer in broad daylight" (as he called fiction writers) cannot explain the source and effect of his or her own creativity. In describing their creative endeavour, poets, writers, artists, and inventors frequently use birth imagery, and metaphors of conception and gestation of the symbolic "baby" (e.g., Coleridge, Wordsworth, Henry James, Nietzsche, Rilke). Hardly surprising, then, that when asked to contemplate the praxis of my own writing, I too drift into procreative imagery. Yet, even at this point, despite twelve books and over a hundred and fifty single-author professional papers (ironically, on Reproduction, the subject of my clinical and academic specialisation), I realise I know not how they were "incubated".

Like many writers, I shied away from navel-gazing to plumb the process. But over the months of writing this investigative chapter, self-examination and unsolicited loss brought me greater comprehension, whilst astounding me.

The psychic placenta

I compare this wordy examination to an ultrasonic gaze into the womb's darkness. Threatening to publicly expose a most private process, "sonographic" interrogation risks prematurely revealing an incompletely formed as-yet-unborn offspring!

Following this train of thought, I envisage an inhibiting anxiety akin to Bloom's "anxiety of influence". *Gestational anxiety*—a fear that external interference in the unknown delicate process might disrupt growth, an impingement causing it to miscarry or malform. Anxiety that investigating the "psychic placenta" which metabolises fleeting ideas and filters emotion would render it insufficient, failing to nourish the "baby" or to rid the womb of its waste products. Anxiety that if, like the imagined foetus, the work belongs to an unchallenged, intensely inventive "intermediate" area of experiencing in which inner reality and external life intermingle—naming the baby too soon will evaporate the mystery. Conversely, there is a fear that having grown inside, once birthed, the ensuing creation will expose more than its creator intended.

So how can I possibly write about my own writing?

As ever, redemption comes from reading. I recalled Hannah Arendt's concept of "natality" (which rang true with the birth of each of my nine grandchildren). To her, every birth promises a new initiative, a potential unpredictable actualisation of freedom through the capacity to act—which means ability to "disclose" oneself to do the unanticipated. Because we are each unique:

> something new is started which cannot be expected from whatever may have happened before. This character of *startling unexpectedness* is inherent in all beginnings… The fact that man [sic] is capable of action means that *the unexpected can be expected* from him, that he is able to perform what is infinitely improbable.
>
> (1958, pp. 177–178, emphases mine)

So will "natality" apply to the act of writing? And, if so, can I permit the unpredictable to unexpectedly emerge in my own?

Inner freedom

Writing about writing, a superb writer writes:

> Writing is finally a series of permissions you give yourself to be expressive in certain ways. To invent. To leap. To fly. To fall. To find your own characteristic way of narrating and insisting; that is, to find your own inner freedom.
>
> (Sontag, 2001, p. 224)

Collecting my thoughts as I begin to try and chart my own "characteristic way of narrating and insisting", I realise this must involve dissolving preconceived ideas. In-the-moment self-scrutiny means introspective invigilation to lay bare personal findings (however selectively they will be later transcribed). But reflecting on the writing process while I write also forces me to *extricate* myself from a fluent experiential happening and slow it down to monitor patterns of formulation as these occur.

Hmmm... this commission to consciously share what takes place unwittingly and in solitude is turning out to be constraining as well as liberating.

The risk and reward are self-discovery. The "improbable" possibility of finding something of "startling unexpectedness" about my own on-going process since I began to write over seventy years ago. Delineating self-given "permissions" entails both retrospectively digging up roots of current work and prospective incentives that may propel me towards future publication. First discovery: my impetus resides in *après coup*. A desire to do better—to further what I missed in previous work.

All seems to be going well, but then disaster occurs, forcing me to scrutinise what makes me persevere with writing despite major obstacles: in the case of this specific chapter—the irretrievable loss of the near-complete work when my hard-drive crashed, and the Dropbox failed to "sync".

'Et in Arcadia ego'

Incredibly, we trust externalising our thoughts to flimsy paper, or fallible screens. Re-reading the little I *have* retained after my now obsolete purple laptop gave up its ghost, I glimpse—as through a glass darkly—the vanished version of this chapter. Striving to ignore blanks where I know text flowed, I am disconcerted by wrongly positioned paragraphs and unmended cavities like hungry moth-holes in the interwoven text. I grasp at word-wisps, but what I wrote then is no longer intact in my memory (precisely because written).

In time, as expensive IT experts make it clear that my frail hope of re-coverability is unsustainable, I face the Porlockian finality of interrupted self-communication.

Eventually I recognise that what is gone cannot be reconstituted. Yet I feel less curious, and less motivated, to rewrite since the writing was already done. Now it is gone, why go on? I suppose because I feel an obligation to the editor of this book who commissioned the article. And to the book's readers. Moreover, to myself.

Wincing as I admit the precious exactitude of a completed text, what comes to mind is Thomasina's poignant "how can we sleep for grief?" (Her *cri de cœur* in Stoppard's play *Arcadia* regarding loss of the precious ancient manuscripts and scrolls destroyed in fires that burned down the Great Library of Alexandria.) My own script was a modest creation. As it resonates with far greater losses in my life, I concede its insignificance in the wider scheme of things.

Grudgingly, I accept the non-productivity of vain attempts to resurrect partially remembered, vaporised text and opaque imagery from the ether where it has dispersed—and decide to begin again...

Yes, the writing task was almost done. But the manuscript I will soon submit is no longer that which existed almost in its entirety some months ago. What you are reading is not even a "guesstimated" reconstruction of the original—but perhaps richer for being crafted within recognition of the finality of loss... *loss can be formative.*

Playing with fire

My very first book was written before I could read.

My mother painstakingly took down dictation of my stories and other "writings", including my first poem:

> When I was only three,
> Daddy catched a star for me,
> And I put it in a matchbox.

Looking back, I ask myself—is *that* the impossible task I have been attempting ever since? Striving to reach the unreachable and catch it in my own match-box/book—as my enabling parents did for me? Do I use my writing to capture and archive stars-words in the hope they will prove inspiring, even incendiary, while recognising that any brief flare is likely to burn out into a twisted, blackened remnant...

What we read are mere sparks. Enlivened deposits from the writer's cumulative past. Imaginative gleanings. Flickering intentions gathered together in a specific place, garnered from a particular inner-world phase. Unpredictably, seemingly dry word-strings can prove prophetic, while freshly minted shiny ones may be already obsolete. Some written words, whether assembled as science, art, or craft, live on borrowed time like stars—extinguished residues of light-years gone by.

Readers may well ask: are written statements just faint nebulous radiations from a brighter sphere whence they originated? Or conversely, is their luminosity all the more intense for being verbally isolated from the sub-symbolic pool? These seem to reflect two schools of thought among writers. Some praise the improved clarity when thinking is distilled through writing. Others, like the contemporary author Mary Gordon, believe that "[N]o marks on paper can ever measure up to the world's music in the mind, to the purity of the image before its ambush by language". Perhaps these reflect different forms of writing.

Either way, writing rarely comes ready-made. For as Nathaniel Hawthorne proclaimed: "[E]asy reading is damn hard writing". Scripted words are not a form of Kabbalistic *yesh me'ayin* materialisation of something from nothing, but constitute the working up (working-through) of flash into flame. Or, to paraphrase Thomas Edison on success: "10% inspiration and 90% perspiration"—or good editing...

But talent figures. To quote David Foster Wallace, himself one of the most extraordinarily talented writers of our time: "Entertainers can divert and engage and maybe even console; only artists can transfigure" (2012, p. 53).

Transcending limitations

It is noteworthy that, historically and developmentally, writing is a late arrival on the art scene. In children, as in prehistoric humanity, proto-writing usually follows on communicative sounds, intelligible speech, and visual representations. Diverse psychoanalysts such as Balint, Bion, Fairbairn, Freud, Klein, Lacan, Winnicott, and others all stress a similar initial catalyst to development of symbolic thought—the infant's recognition of a *gap* or *lack* or *absence*. Whether motivated by a desire to preserve, share, or repair, art, from abstract engravings in Blombos cave dating back seventy thousand years, through rock-face depictions by non-literate cultures such as the African /Xam bushmen or later Egyptian wall engravings, allows us to glimpse ancient beliefs, myths, and rituals. Was it threat of imminent loss that incited early artists to eternalise what felt most precarious? Were certain aspects of their lives depicted on protected ledges to proclaim ownership or as notation for other nomads? And once verbal utterance was transmuted to shapes, what induced them to supplement pictures with cartouched hieroglyphs, cuniform, or other squiggles?

Archaeological evidence suggests that spoken language already existed around 35,000 BCE, but the earliest written symbols found to date go back only some six to seven thousand years. As numbers seem to pre-date alphabet by many thousand years, one supposition for the leap is mundane: *record-keeping.* But another major incentive is *narrative communication.* Myriad letter-patterns preserved over the millennia—whether etched on clay or stone, penned on papyrus, silk, or pottery, on walls or gold-embossed and wooden coffins—were intended for others: to spell out important events, name brave actions, announce news or share gossip, to specify accounts, scribe poems, or tell stories. *Writing provides an arc that transcends time and space, overriding personal boundaries and limitations of experience.*[1]

Generative agency

Whatever its original meanings, symbolism is *evidence of an imagination* grappling to convey or retain an ephemeral vision. Winnicott located the production of human culture in a "transitional space", like that in which children feel free to expand their boundaries in unself-conscious creativity. He likened this protected zone wherein feelings can be reworked to the safety of being "alone in the presence of the mother" during states of early quasi-symbolic play (1967). Freud, too, deemed adult creativity to be "a continuation of, and a substitute for, what was once the play of childhood" (1908e, p. 152), noting the survival of both its "intense seriousness" and the "yield of pleasure" derived from it (p. 144). And he declared that, conversely, "every child at play behaves like a creative writer, in the sense that he creates a world of his own" (p. 143), expressing deepest yearnings and unsatisfied wishes in imaginative form. Elsewhere (Raphael-Leff, 2010), I tried to answer the question this poses—why, if most children play imaginatively, do so few remain creators in adulthood?

My take is that early awareness of one's creative capacity—"generative identity" as I termed it—is forged alongside growing awareness of *constraints* (of sameness, diversity, complementarity, and inequalities of age, gender, race, class, family variations). These arise in the context of exploring oedipal distinctions of gender (embodiment, representation, desire).

Greenacre famously asserted that toddlers engage in "a love affair with the world". But close observation reveals that this expansive phase of exuberant belief that one can do or be anything is short-lived. To my mind, serious disillusionment sets in as a young child's omnipotence collapses by confrontation with the basic facts of life. These facts incorporate insurmountable restrictions—of *sex* (I can be only male or female), *genesis* (not self-made but reproduced by two others), *generativity* (females can gestate; males impregnate), *generation* (only adults procreate), and *genitive anxieties* (of separateness, arbitrariness, irreversibility, and finitude). Compensation lies in the future—a promise of eventual adult power and a baby of their own.

However, I maintain that this new awareness of one's own generative identity also allows the child to make a momentous shift from being someone else's creation or creature to being a potential pro-creator—or even *creator*. As frustrations, dilemmas, anxieties, and previous identifications are reworked through imaginative play, some children employ their *agential capacity* to transcend restrictions, absence, and loss, while others daydream or succumb to limitations. Complying with polarised gender stereotypes, and socially permissible rule-bound games, originality may be inhibited by dread of a castrating response. Dissatisfied, another child defies restrictions through intellectual or physical prowess. One who retains pre-oedipal omnipotence may rebel by denying or disavowing one or more facts of life. Another finds an ingenious solution—both coming to terms with facts yet playing with the impossible, by creatively generating "a world of his own".

Creativity involves both accepting limitations and recapturing the sense of being "everything". Mitigating rational acquiescence to fact with transcendence of constraints of age, anatomy, and biological

determinism by cultivating a spectrum of characteristics including imaginatively being procreative mother and father.

Dreaming the impossible

Due to the new reality of possessing a fertile sexual body capable of actual impregnation/ childbearing, generative identity must be reworked in
adolescence. Puberty floridly reactivates the sense of omnipotent invin-
cibility and restrictions in new fantasies, which may be anxiously curbed
or defiantly played out. Modifying reality and discovering who one is
now usually involves new forms of play, including fantasy games where
megalomania is given free rein. Active experimentation is often accom-
panied by typical teenage risk-taking and toddler-like tantrums as well
as creative "out of the box" thinking and imaginative free-play. In revising generative identity, some adolescents may focus on the virtual realm.
Others thrive on live adventurous excitement, including thrill-seeking of
forbidden intellectual, sexual, or drug-induced knowledge or powerful
physical violence. Yet others prematurely satisfy the futuristic promise
of procreativity, or resolve to concretely fulfil aspirations to change their
bodily shape or sex.

   But teenagers who can tolerate uncertainty, ambiguity, and incongru-
ity within the self may dare to challenge the impossible. Those who can
envisage themselves as "creators" find innovative intellectual or artistic
ways to express their generative agency by transforming their visions and
multiple identifications into substantive original creations *designed to en-
dure beyond ephemeral play.* I stress "dare" because, although tremen-
dously enjoyable, invention is always open to perturbations. The activity
of "dreaming by daylight" is not anxiety-free, since all creativity—art,
dance, music, literature, sculpture, science—begins with an ineffable
gap. A blank page, raw ingredients, and a demanding enigma to explore.
Furthermore, the creative act requires finding the courage to hold at bay
anxieties while simulating those archaic procreative parents symbolically. My thesis is that the degree to which we can retain accessibility
to our early expansive state of imaginatively believing we can do or be
anything, forms and informs the substrate of creativity. But then again,
so does its reception.

Writing and reading

Some texts fail to hold the reader's attention or threaten to be too
arousing. Creativity is thus compounded by the recipient's take, which
can vary from highly critical to accepting or unquestioningly gullible.
Writers and their readers are inextricably bridged by the text, which for
both may permit, or even invite, fuller articulation of unknown facets of

our selves. Freud puzzled over the author's ignorance of how his/her imagination manages "to make such an impression on us… and to arouse in us emotions, of which, perhaps, we had not even thought ourselves capable" (Freud, 1908e, p. 143). Many writers have tried to solve this riddle, including psychoanalyst Ron Britton, who says: "Much of the emotional power of great fiction lies in its ability to evoke and work through unconscious phantasy" (1998, p. 113).

To my mind, evocative power lies neither in content nor specific mode of delivery (structure, form, style of presentation, linguistic array of expressive tropes and metaphors) but in the work as an *affective bridge*. When author and reader walk in unison across it, in matching rhythmicity and sensual pacing—the bridge sways as affinities resonate in deep semiotic reverberations. Getting "lost" in reading happens through such unconscious resonance.

If writing provides access to happenings beyond our own experience, it also provides intimate access to an author's mind. His or her values, wishes, fantasies, intuitions, and mode of reasoning; memories and influences, and the multiplicity of cross-sex and other identifications that become evident through portrayal of a range of gendered characters and the interplay of their many voices (see Dostoyevsky!). When attuned, the reader who partakes of these basic sympathies can learn to apprehend, even anticipate, the writer's intentions. She or he shares in a growing compilation of essential meanings resembling a *dyadic state of consciousness*, such as develops between especially close confidantes. (Hence in the shockwaves following Foster Wallace's unanticipated death, readers were forced to recall that their writer, who had vowed to go on communicating what it felt like to be human or die trying, had also proclaimed that the reader cannot read your mind (2013).)

But the author, too, is a reader. Good writing is embedded in reading good books. As Susan Sontag claimed "to write is to practice, with particular intensity and attentiveness, the art of reading" (2001, p. 225). A reader may be permeable to self-exploration at this moment in time, but less receptive to the same text later. Reading, too, reflects an assortment of defences against internal and external pressures. While one reader is captivated by the page-turning momentum, another is stand-offishly disinterested or wary to the point of breaking off engagement. Overly conscientious readers meticulously register every word; less careful ones often slip-slide within a text, skipping lines or whole paragraphs, as impatient for resolution they rush headlong to the close.

Critical propensities vary too. Some take the author's equivocations and frailties for granted. Others reverberate to suppressed imagery, or strain to sniff out secrets hidden within the crevices. Subjectivity creeps in to reading. As therapists, we know from consulting room experience that, however unbiased we believe ourselves to be, our interpretations are replete with psycho-historical and current preoccupations. This applies even to so-called impartial critics who, as Northorp Frye pointed out, inevitably judge literary works on the basis of their own ideology. But he adds, "[T]he axiom of criticism must be, not that the poet does not know what he is talking about, but that he cannot talk about what he knows" (1957, p. 5).

A double whammy! Not only is the wordsmith gagged by the very act of writing, but each reader then rewrites the manuscript!

Hence, the self-same material diverges subtly in meaning from that read by another reader, or dredges up more for the same reader at a different time. Furthermore, the written text itself is never fully static or transparent but morphs or compresses as it matures, rejuvenates, or outdates. Literally so these days, when e-texts allow for constant amendments, as meanings destabilise, transmute and re-form to keep pace with altered world experience of the author and each new cohort of readers.

So, paradoxically, whether words are illuminations of obscurity or impoverished reductions from greater clarity—as an author retraces the transcriptive process between mind and page of thoughts transitioning to written word—the edited script we rely upon is already inert. It will only re-acquire its dynamism from the reader's input.

Even more paradoxically, in re-reading my own work I myself am no longer just author but become reader, altering the text through my own critical gaze (and editorial cut-and-paste). But like any other reader, I inevitably tap into my subjectivity, perhaps especially so when interrogating my own personal transformative process. We may ask whether indeed, for a writer, is objective "exteriority" even tolerable? Or does (as Simon Critchley asserts with reference to Blanchot) some "incommunicable dread" induce a moment of bad faith that creeps in to protect us from its truth (2004, p. 34)? An enactment of fragmentation; a use of irony, wit, or intellectual mystification as refusal of full comprehension of what we have written…

Conversely, how can we ever fully convey the pleasure yield of writing? Wonder at the flow, the heightened sense of artistry, the day- and dreamtime ongoing preoccupation that subsides into quiet insouciance on a project's completion. The tense insularity needed to protect deep-set absorption, all senses alert and bristling in raised curiosity. Even now, as I look up while typing these words, I find myself enthralled to the writing, having lost track of time…

Message in a bottle

In writing here, I wanted to draw a distinction between professional and personal writing, but within the framework of psychoanalytic thinking this strict dichotomy cannot hold. We all agree that in an apprenticeship profession such as psychotherapy, process notes and practice-oriented scientific papers are supremely educational. Nonetheless, while well-intentioned, some facets may seem transgressive. For instance, overly disguising the protagonist or, conversely, revealing too much—too dispassionate, or over-involved. Furthermore, writing a paper during the course of an ongoing therapy also often disrupts clinical progress as the analyst's finely attuned free-floating attention inexorably hones in on manifestations of the topic in mind. By its very nature, capturing the patient's words on paper converts *ephemeral into permanent*, while publication renders the confidential public. And portrayal pins down the dynamic experience of an elusive, always only partially known, other.

So if writing grants freedom to sky-glide, it carries dangers beyond suddenly falling flat on one's face. Some writers protect themselves by using a talisman-pen, keeping disciplined hours, minimising distractions in an insulated and set place, a special private studio or study—a "room of one's own". In an attempt to combat blocks and reign in the dreaded uncontrollable, some writers even self-impose imaginary deadlines. My own experience is the opposite—when obligations pressurise, I baulk at the untimeliness, the struggle to retrieve, garner, discard, or even make sense of ideas fished before their time.

I have always wished to write as and where the spirit takes me—to grasp a dream sliver on waking, on a bus, or in a market-place, grab an errant image hoping it won't float away uncaptured on the page. While swimming, I try to hang on to the brain-wave fizzing in my mind before the fragile bubble pops. Lest it seems easy, as many fiction writers attest, words and the cast of characters do not simply do our bidding. Even sentences have a life of their own. Some are netted ready-made, scaled, finned, and sparkling, while others surface from the depths trailing bits of seaweed and dredged-up refuse. Some must be actively trawled, stirring up the flotsam and jetsam of the mind, while the most recalcitrant hide on the sea-bed, flatly refusing to emerge out of the internal morass until fully grown.

Meta-metabolism

As suggested, writing offers a form of verbal processing that may draw on early carer–child reflective–digestive work (or, in some cases, compensation for its absence). I suppose the term "mentalization" (Fonagy et al., 2002) is applicable to such literary meta-metabolising—thinking about our own feelings and human behaviour in terms of intentional mental states—needs, desires, beliefs, purposes, and reasons. Peter Hobson proposes that a child's growing capacity to change perspectives and see things from the other's point of view indicates a new form of self-consciousness—of being a "self among other selves" rather than the centre of the world (2002, p. 255). I suggest that the process of creative writing similarly veers between egoistic and other-centred perspectives. When playful ingenuity overrides regurgitation, writing may take off as an imaginative flight fuelled by curiosity. "It is in playing and only in playing that the child or adult is able to be creative and to use the whole personality, and it is only in being creative that the individual discovers the self", says impish Winnicott (1971, p. 54).

To me, with acquisition of literacy, the generative desire to write seems to unfold on three levels:

- An anxiety-provoking emotional experience or unspeakable raw state of experiential elation, confusion, or painful deficit.
- Temporary suspension of strict in–out/fact–fiction divisions and openness to plunder and explore myriad facets and identifications within his/her own mind (play), enables the writer to transcend the flurry of overwhelming immediacy.
- A self-observed *re*-representational state when the processed experience now transfigured in tangible or abstract symbolic form, generates a new level of awareness, viewed from a relatively detached standpoint in which the author's empathy can hold the reader's mind in mind.

So, creative representation allows us to digest and distil experience. It preserves events against forgetfulness but also imaginatively transfigures reality. While transgenerational story-telling and oral history aid live remembrance of glorious deeds to become sources of inspiration, and pictorial representations enhance culture, writing fixes in fine detail dynamic moments of perishable thought, realising complex ideas, bringing together new patterns of concepts and feelings. Fiction goes further to transport us across time, place, and person.

In sum, written formulations transmit *mind to mind in absentia.*

I am not with you as you read this. And yet my words are.

The multiplexity of writing

Writing straddles a continuum from intimate contemplation in a personal journal to something intended for select social media or indiscriminate distribution. I realise that whether private or public, journalistic or creative, relating fact, fantasy, or fiction—the common denominator is that *writing anchors transient thoughts.* All else varies.

The mode of production may be slow, laboured, and reflective, or urgent to capture the world's snap-crackle-pop before it turns soggy. Subject matter may draw on personal, academic, or historical truths, may originate from a reliable source of information or in today's parlance of false, fake, or alternative facts, one of manipulative mendacity.

Assuming their imagined reader's viewpoint, some authors try to supply order. Others strive to avoid judgement of an overly condensed narrative as resistance or failure of imagination. If some writers fear violation of their integrity by culling the stream of consciousness, others fear that a text's opinionated certainty will raise the reader's heckles. Self-examination reveals my own concern that my reader may feel cheated by clarifying yet over-simplistic arguments that deny the multifaceted nature of the mind. Hence this somewhat convoluted, overly dense text...

Incentives to create may reflect a lack, a need to share, desire for reparation, preservation, restored emotional equilibrium, or recognition. The impetus to write is driven by mixed vectors ranging from self-clarification or cathartic discharge, ideological persuasion or aspiration to impart a serious testament, or even to provide frivolous entertainment. Writing as a conduit of self-expression, or seeking recognition, even rousing activist demonstration—the final product often surprises in its intricate mixture of conscious intent with unexpected consequences. Similarly, literary styles lie on a broad spectrum from scholarly and academic via factual, descriptive, or reflective means all the way to vividly imaginative, boundary-shifting narrative, even visionary and transcending the possible. But variations occur even within a defined "band". For instance, Hanna Segal distinguished the "as-if" world of fantasy fiction that serves escapism from the "what-if" fiction that requires exploratory reckoning of what occurs if a parameter is changed (1991, p. 107). In short, a piece of writing can take many shapes—scientific-pragmatic article to poem, play, short story, novel, or book, across many genres—romantic to satirical, dramatic to scholarly, epic, tragic, or a multi-axial admixture of them all.

But whatever its overt goal, given the complex cluster of conscious and unconscious motivations and human fallibility, each moment of writing may constitute an act of courage and/or betrayal that risks succumbing to self-indulgence, complacent negligence, or pitfalls of self- or other-deception...

Above all, writing is a *testament of being*: "I EXIST is the signal that throbs under most voluntary writing—and all good writing" stated David Foster Wallace (2012, p. 82) not long before his suicide.

Obviously, such long-distance communication is not interchangeable with direct speech, which has a sensual power that script lacks. Moment-by-moment non-conscious tracking of subsymbolic cues enhance the exchange, offering a potential means of both getting "into" and *modifying* the other's experience. In-the-flesh exchanges, whether in a dialogic twosome or group, the speaker's audible emotional tonality and identifiable voice is absorbed into the listener's sensorium. Participants unconsciously fathom each other's feelings by experiencing them. So, vocality and bodily presence allow for potential resonance irrespective of the purpose of the exchange—a chat or helpful discussion, educational transmission of tradition; gossip-exchange, an investigative encounter, or menacing interrogation; factual testimony, inspirational story-telling, or poignant self-account. A direct face-to-face encounter evokes unconscious registers by appealing directly to our shared humanity. As the philosopher Levinas wrote: "The face [is] a source from which all meaning appears", exposing us to the reality of the other as a separate vulnerable "living presence"—beyond our control or full understanding (*Totality and Infinity*, p. 297).

By contrast, what is written may try to convey a "living presence" but usually involves *a distanced* reception of the writer's thoughts and ideas. And addressing an imaginary reader or an unknown mass, or even a particular real recipient, typically we write to one who is *not there*. In turn, the script is often read in the writer's absence. But even when read out aloud by its author, it is already transmuted from voice to page and back. That said, writing can slow down and apply a fine-grained descriptive mesh, divulging in words what is intuitively sensed yet omitted from consciousness.

Writing is legacy. Writing, whether ancient archaeological or indelible Facebook "postings", hails from a particular temporal and spatial locus. Similarly, reading is invested with contemporary preoccupations. Since the reader's responsive intake is at one remove, *the text is always already subject to internal amendments and external updates.*

As I well know, even for the writer, understanding often comes *après-coup*—as characters and content write themselves. Furthermore, as Derrida phrases it, the author rarely holds the *key* to the text since the written always "defers" its meaning. We are complex beings. The notion of "deconstruction" contends that meanings always shift and contain traces of prior meanings that will also accrue different meanings with time (Derrida, 1978). In any text, there are inevitably points of equivocation and undecidability that betray a stable determinate meaning that an author might seek to impose upon his or her text.

Ultimately, I cannot be sure what I have written.

Self-discovery

So finally, writing is a fundamental pathway to exploring what I think.

Crucially, as a form of self-analysis (and remember, Freud's own analysis was a written one), writing promises a mode of private deliberation to process feelings and ideas, a treasure trove to rummage in, and an unconstrained rehearsal of new perceptions. Irrespective of its overt intention, aims, and significance, beginning a piece of original writing instigates (and is instigated by) a self-reflective search usually motivated by hope of better understanding—and receptivity to the unanticipated. Arendt's statement: "*startling unexpectedness is inherent in all beginnings…*"

In sum, generative agency expresses itself in multiple ways. I know writers who claim to arrive at the sitting with a complete mental text ready to be typed. Others wallow in months of unfettered exploration or the agony of facing a blank page. Ill-content with "half knowledge", some creators strive for certitude and closure, while others trust in "the heart's perceptions", allowing "negative capability" to play a major role ("... being in uncertainties, Mysteries, doubts, without any irritable reaching after fact and reason", John Keats wrote to his brother George on Sunday, 21 December 1817).

Some writers experience the prohibitive weight of previous creators in "anxiety of influence" (Bloom, 1973). Others, suffering what I called "gestational anxiety", fear disruptions of the creative process itself. Anxieties may focus on premature exposure or blockage, liminality or personal disclosure—putting a creation out in public among strangers to be misunderstood or harshly judged. Or, anxiety may relate to un-leashing chaotic forces within—metaphorically envisaged as whirlpools or witchery, volcanos, tsunamis, thin ends of the rational wedge... Or the unconscious conflation of creation and forbidden procreation.

My writing?

My writing has its own momentum. Some of it has miraculously flowed in that "intermediary" state where originality can flourish. At other times, ideas jotted down hastily on the backs of used envelopes serendipitously make an appearance when needed...

Writing offers a means of rich dialogue between me and myself, and self-nourished replenishment. But it also offers a sense of communing with other writers I value. When, in creative solitude, I pull back and catch sight of myself inserting words into the script, my singularity seems a given, even while outwitted by new imaginaries. I write in a state of intense yet relaxed concentration. But the process is not a consistent one. Only if I manage to hold on to indistinct thoughts and tolerate raw stuff emerging can I venture to stretch the boundaries of what is already known to me.

So far from obeying a fixed rationale, I find my overall schema be-gins to unravel in the course of writing. Oxymoronically, flexibility is imperative. However carefully planned, at least for me, composition of a "creation" is a *non-linear progression* that transpires not in a vacuum but through constant renegotiation with internal as well as external forces, susceptible to digressions, inspirations, and interruptions. As it unfolds, my roadmap takes on a directional life of its own, even when I am writing a purely didactic text.

At first, I read enthusiastically and somewhat indiscriminately, plac-ing and testing my own thinking in the context of a diversity of opinions.

As my comprehension broadens and clarifies, I start writing, but try to remain open to new ideas which break through the blueprint. And having re-read what I have written, my "daylight dreaming" is interspersed with night-time pre-sleep reflections. Resembling tapestry-making, diversely coloured multi-threaded strands of thought leap across their discrete textual categories to become interwoven with criss-crossing filaments of imagery, creating new interlacing and unexpected knots and bobbles embedded in the embroidered script.

So while this interim process of self-discovery allows a flow of personal associations to play itself out, the outpouring can only be provisional and, before long, I as author must engage in an editing process to pare it down from wild over-inclusive or vague ramblings, to try and provide coherence for the reader. As the process of writing itself begins to dissolve distorting incrustations, fixed habits of thought and accepted rules of academia may fall by the wayside, giving way to something fresh. But eventually the critical 'I' must take over to transform it into readable stuff.

Private introspection and idiosyncratic thinking give way to critical judgement, retrospective assessment, and the test of commonality. I re-read, critique, and edit, occupying multiple roles—of originator, monitor, and recipient—because my grasp of the work is affected by the very act of grappling with perplexing ideas, and trying to illuminate their ineffable meanings in writing. That is why my lost text was irrecoverable. I cannot, under different conditions, recreate those previous transpositions of interleaving ideas. On the other hand, I am eternally grateful for word-processing ideally suited to this fluidity—which felt so irksome when typewriting's cut-and-paste were literal, and Tipp-Ex liberal...

And then suddenly, miraculously, it is over.
I could re-read, tweak, add, or amend, but I have no further desire to.
I have learned that pluri-motivated and multi-faceted, writing is a crucial part of my life.
A font of new understandings, albeit subject to constant internal shifts and revisions.
Imperfect as this is, it is done—so now it is over to you, the reader.

Note

1 The first known written "letter" is a cuneiform clay-tablet from 2400 BCE, sent by the high-priest Lu'enna to the King of Lagash (maybe Urukagina), informing him of his son's death in combat (found in Telloh, ancient Girsu in Mesopotamia, today's Iraq). The earliest known literary text is a poem written by an Akkadian/Sumerian woman by the name of Enheduanna (2285–2250 BCE), daughter of Saragon the Great. And first books?

The Egyptian Book of the Dead, was recorded in the Papyrus of Ani around 1240 BCE (but other versions of the book probably date from about the 18th century BCE). And in ancient Mesopotamia, *Hammurabi's Code,* dates back to around 1754 BCE. Preserved on a massive basalt stone stele well over two metres tall and various clay tablets, it does not quite meet our conventional criteria of a book (but then, neither does an e-book), but it is one of the oldest and most important deciphered writings of significant length in the world, consisting of 282 basic Babylonian tenets of Law regarding contracts, transactions, official obligations, household and family relationships which provide a window onto a lost world.

Chapter 11

Writing as rebellion

Morris Nitsun

I begin with a bold assertion: many of the great writers have been rebels. Pushing the frontiers of any field of writing requires courage and determination. Whether in literature, science, or the arts and cultural studies, those who have made the greatest impact have usually stood apart from convention and dared to challenge long-standing assumptions and beliefs. If this applies to those who achieve greatness and wield profound influence, it at the same time reflects an aspect of the wider universe of writers who struggle to contribute something original or novel, often coming from the margins of society but seeking to communicate insights that might illuminate an aspect of the world they inhabit. The act of writing itself may be seen as rebellious. Separating oneself from the majority, often in states of withdrawal or isolation, not unusually for many months if not years, requires an independent spirit, a willingness to forego some of the easier pleasures and comforts of living. Most writers regard it as a difficult profession. Apart from the uncertain outcome of a piece of writing, particularly for those struggling to achieve a basic level of success, it separates them from the mainstream, while they at the same time seek to be recognised and appreciated. In itself, this is a dilemma: how to rebel, to be different, to comment from the outside, yet to be accepted and valued.

I write from my experience not as a professional writer whose sole occupation is writing but as a practising psychologist, psychotherapist, and group analyst who has written for most of my career and whose books and articles have achieved some recognition within my chosen field. Having an over-arching profession such as psychology / psychotherapy, gives me the luxury of earning my living in an altogether more reliable and consistent way, while allowing me to contribute as a writer and to observe the experience as a participant. My interest in motivation and the way human beings express themselves, their challenges and constraints, offers me insights into my own writing process, my relationship to writing, and that of fellow-writers to their craft. Further, I am an artist, having painted, exhibited, and sold my work over several decades, and this gives me additional insights into the pleasures and tensions of the creative process.

In this chapter, I focus on my own writing as rebellion within the sphere of group analysis. I am aware that some readers may be unfamiliar with group analysis. But this is my institutional home, one that I refer to throughout this chapter, and I hope that readers will be sufficiently interested to follow my journey. Having qualified as a group analyst at the Institute of Group Analysis in 1990 and as a training group analyst in 2006, I have been committed to working in therapeutic groups and organisations for many years. Most of this work has been stimulating and rewarding and my identity as a group analyst has grown correspondingly through the decades. However, most of what I have written has challenged some basic aspects of group analysis, particularly the theoretical frame developed by S. H. Foulkes in the mid-twentieth century and his followers later in the century. This has presented me with the immediate problem of wanting to speak my voice to my colleagues and the wider profession, wanting to be free to convey my concerns and criticisms, honestly and unflinchingly, but also wanting to be part of the profession, to be included and recognised. It is difficult to judge the extent to which this has been achieved. There are times when my clinical work, my theoretical arguments, and my collegial relationships have felt integrated, at one, but other times when I have felt in conflict with myself, in uneasy alliance with my profession, and uncomfortable with my position as a rebel in the field. I continue to feel subject to contradictory messages of admiration and admonition, recognised and ignored, included and excluded. I suspect that I am not alone, not necessarily in the sense that many others are outwardly rebellious, but that some tensions between conformity and non-conformity are germane to any developing field of science, applied science, and the arts. These tensions are sometimes expressed in writing: other times they are more hidden. But, either way, I suggest, they occupy a significant part of the thinking and feeling of practitioners in a specific field. Rebel writers tend to give voice to the concerns that others may harbour but are reluctant to express or put into the public domain. I suggest that to do so is an achievement, to state one's case clearly and unambiguously. There is usually a measure of appreciation from one's colleagues that accrues from this, but also a degree of distancing and repudiation, as if the rebellious thought must be silenced and relegated to the writer and not the field as such. This may leave the writer feeling alone, with a painful sense of exclusion, possibly even experiencing guilt and shame for making what may feel like a destructive attack.

Background

Group analysis was originated in Europe by S. H. Foulkes, a German Jewish psychiatrist and psychoanalyst who sought refuge from the Nazis in England in 1932. Foulkes himself was a rebel. A Freudian psychoanalyst by training, he remained loyal to his roots in most respects. However, by initiating group analysis, he significantly changed the frame of intervention from the traditional individual setting to the radical group setting, from the couch to the circle (Schlapobersky, 2016). The psychoanalytic establishment at the time did not take kindly to this change. There was considerable resistance to group psychotherapy, and Foulkes had a major battle on his hands that resulted in some estrangement from the psychoanalytic community and to a lesser degree from the psychiatric establishment of which he remained a part. His own writing did not reflect this to any great degree. His publications were not his strength: his writing is a mixture of prosaic and muddled that left group analysis an incomplete and somewhat confused discipline. But there was enough in his writing to bolster the new approach and, in spite of the ambivalent reception, the discipline strengthened in years to come.

One of the consequences of Foulkes' struggle, I have suggested (Nitsun, 1996) was the tendency to present what I regard as an idealised and over-optimistic view of group analysis. For example, he described the group as "the most powerful therapeutic agency known to us" (Foulkes, 1964, p. 76). This was not backed by research then or even now, at least partly because the complexity of the group psychotherapy process makes it very difficult to subject to evaluation and research. Linked to this, there was in his writing, in my view, an absence, if not avoidance, of the most problematic aspects of group membership and behaviour. Hostility and aggression, both in the group and towards the group, hardly featured in his writing. The result, as I have written about quite extensively, was a largely one-sided picture of the group, one that contrasted with the more challenging theories of Bion (1961), who emphasised the deep ambivalence people have about group membership as well as the regressive aspects of the group. This resulted in a split between Bion's followers and those of Foulkes, with the group field becoming demarcated along the lines of a "structure of opposition" (Dews, 1987), tending to polarise the optimistic and pessimistic visions of the group. This dilemma was the stimulus for my early writing as a group analyst. I found myself taking a challenging position, leading me to formulate the concept of the anti-group, the area of discourse for which I am probably best known as a writer. My purpose in formulating the concept was not to highlight negative or destructive group processes for their own sake, but to consider how these forces undermined group development and limited the creativity of the group: with this understanding, we might facilitate the full potential of the group. This was my first rebellion. Whether in fact it counts as rebellion is a debatable point—there is a difference between rebellion and challenge or criticism, especially where criticism has some foundation, but the two may easily be confused.

There were other themes that were marginalised in Foulkes' writing or that were formulated in a distinctive, slanted way. One concerned authority and leadership. Foulkes is admired within the field for his vision of the group "conductor" as a democratic leader, not a leader with authoritarian intentions but a leader who led from behind, who transferred authority from himself to the group (Foulkes, 1964). In this, too, Foulkes was himself a rebel, departing from the vertical mode of authority inherent in the classical psychoanalytic position to a horizontal mode of authority. However, as with many foundational theories, this formulation in my view became reified, if not deified, and failed to recognise the more complex dynamics of authority relations in which a firm but fair authority is needed developmentally and where the conflict with authority may be germane for development. This was a further stimulus for my own writing as a rebel (Nitsun, 2009, 2015).

The third area that was marginalised in group analysis, beginning with Foulkes and continuing into the present, was sexuality. Sexuality itself was virtually absent from Foulkes' writing, and even more so the overall context of desire in which sexuality is embedded—desire as a deeper and wider consideration, as a life force that propels us as human beings. Yet, without offering an open discourse on sexuality, not only was the exploration of sex marginalised but assumptions made about sexual diversity that no longer tally with contemporary views and that create a normative and sometimes pathologising account of difference. That sexuality—and desire more generally—are powerfully present in some form in groups is indisputable but equally the need for a discourse in theory and practice. Here, too, I took up the challenge and also responded in writing (Nitsun, 2006).

Writing and publication anxiety

The dynamics of the writer as rebel arise in a complex matrix in which there is anxiety at several levels of the creative process. There is first of all anxiety about writing itself. People vary considerably in their confidence as writers. Although in my chosen fields of psychology, psychotherapy, and group analysis, there are many excellent writers, seemingly confident and able to assert their creativity, I know of numerous colleagues who regard writing with trepidation. There appear to be various sources of anxiety. Am I able to write creatively? Am I literate and fluent enough with the written word to risk it? What will emerge? Will it be a mess? What will I reveal about myself? Do I have anything (new) to say? How will people react to my writing, judge me as a writer: consider me foolish and inadequate to the task or, very surprisingly, consider me great? The latter possibility is both desired and feared because of the envy and expectation it may generate.

Both the desire for recognition and the anxiety are intensified by the prospect of publication since this puts the writer's value directly to the test. There is now a ready-made audience that will respond one way or the other to the publication and this is often unpredictable, even for seasoned writers with an established reputation. Britton (1997), in an insightful account of the perils of publication, suggests that publication anxiety is ubiquitous. The main source of this anxiety, he suggests, is a fear of criticism and repudiation by those who hold authority in the field and a fear of rejection and disaffiliation from colleagues with whom the author wishes to be affiliated. These fears are so great that they may altogether inhibit the publication of written work or the presentation of the ideas in a public forum. Even when the inhibition does not go this far, Britton suggests that the work may be distorted by the dynamic relationship of the author to the fantasied audience. This includes an over-readiness to publish, where caution is thrown to the winds, possibly generated by an over-confident belief in the importance of the writing and an over-valuation of the assumed originality of the ideas, with intimations of priestly or prophetic power. So widespread is the anxiety about publication, Britton argues, that not to suffer the anxiety suggests an out-of-touch mentality with a manic edge.

The dynamic that Britton omits, rather surprisingly for a Kleinian psychoanalyst, is envy. Publication is an important and valued part of professional development, a high-status activity, the written word reflecting not only the vision and skill of the writer but potentially influencing the entire culture of the discipline, its institutional home, and its future development. Successful writers usually gain prominence in their fields and this is often augmented by recognition in other countries, invitations to travel and lecture abroad adding to the glamour of the enterprise. Best-selling authors of course may acquire further celebrity status, which even if questionable in some cases or onerous for others, may exacerbate envy. I add envy to the cocktail of publication anxieties as I think it is the configuration of anxiety about rejection and repudiation plus the wish for, and fear of, envy that makes this such a potent brew. The additional difficulty with envy is its invisibility. Although envy can be powerful and destructive in its intent, if not enactment, it is difficult to pinpoint and address in an open way. Its hidden dimension adds to its power.

I highlight these implications of writing and publication to further question the role of the writer as rebel. How does he/she position himself in this dense arena? What are the underlying motives of the rebel? What does he/she hope to gain? I am aware of the complexity of my own motives. I believe that my primary motive is to challenge the omissions and discrepancies in my chosen field, which to some extent I associate with a kind of injustice—the injustice of inequality assigned to certain human topics, the injustice of over-valuing one way of thinking at the expense of another, the injustice of identity built on the dubious validity of theory. But I am aware that this is not the whole picture—that there are my own more narcissistic motives and a very personal struggle with recognition and acceptance, plus envy both as felt from others and towards others. Perhaps the rebel writer instigates a particular courtship with an audience that plays out in unpredictable, sometimes complementary and sometimes contradictory ways. Further, at what point in the history of a given disciples does the writer present his/her view, particularly when those views might destabilise an established orthodoxy? Entering the fray at a sensitive transitional period in the development of the discipline—or helping to generate a fray—intensifies the stakes and the sense of risk.

Oedipal perspectives

I have postulated above that both the drive and anxiety associated with writing and publication can be understood in oedipal terms. If this is true for writers in general, it is all the more true for the rebel writer. There is first of all the generational aspect: the writer with new or challenging ideas is likely either to be of the younger generation or to represent a point of view that departs from the conventions of the parent generation. This cannot but stir up the oedipal dynamics of loyalty versus disloyalty. In my own case, I was aware from the beginning of my difficulty with Foulkes as a symbolic father. In spite of similarities to my own father, including the flight from persecution as Jews and the loss of family in the Holocaust, I found Foulkes difficult to identify with as a figurehead. Whether it was his "betrayal" of his root identity (German Jewish) through changing his name several times, his muddled writing, his omission of crucial areas of discourse, or his idealisation of his product, group analysis—or indeed his success and veneration from others—I do not know. However, my need to rebel reflected an impatience with the founding father and a wish to establish a different, more robust, more realistic approach to groups, as I saw it. To this day, though, while aware that this verges on the irrational, I sometimes feel that I have committed a crime.

In my Foulkes Lecture (Nitsun, 2009), I suggested that the trauma of Foulkes' sudden death while running a group of his successors, the next generation of group analysts, resulted in a failure to mourn his loss and a guilty absorption of his beliefs and identity into the culture of group analysis. I further suggested that the ambivalence about his authority, of which there is published evidence, was dealt with by the reification of his theories. Amongst other consequences, this perpetuated Foulkes' own democratic notions of group leadership, with the core principle of the leader dispensing with his own authority: a worthy contribution but deserving of greater debate than had so far been the case.

This touches on Freud's primal horde theory of group development. In essence, the sons' murder of the father through jealousy of his power evokes guilt that prompts the brothers to unite in reverence for the dead father.

This, symbolically, creates the new religion or ideology. The guilty shadow of the past demands loyalty to the father's tradition. In its extreme forms, it is this conformity that produces cult movements and fundamentalist thinking. At the same time, fundamentalism entails a violent rebellion against any authority or orthodoxy that conflicts with the chosen one.

Reactions to the rebel

In the thirty years or so of my writing as a group analyst, my journey has been marked by reactions from my colleagues that have in turn gratified, delighted, overwhelmed, confused, baffled, disturbed, and troubled me deeply. I struggle with the contradictions. My first paper on the anti-group (Nitsun, 1991) set the tone. Unexpectedly, it was the recipient that year of the Fernando Arroyave Essay Prize for an essay that challenged some basic assumption in Foulkes' theory. In response to the essay, a well-known American group psychotherapist, Saul Tuttman (1996), described the paper as an "historical and ideological breakthrough". He corroborated that, in his view, Foulkes' theory had indeed avoided or denied the darker, destructive potential of groups. Another reviewer, Jerome Gans, described it as "a classic in the field". My paper, and subsequently the book, attracted much attention in the field, and I received many invitations in the UK and abroad to lecture on the subject. But other reviewers were sceptical. Figures in the group analytic institute who once seemed well disposed to me took against my writing—and, it seemed, me. A senior supervisory figure, who had been supportive and appreciative for years, reacted with indignation to my publications, insisting that there was no such thing as the anti-group, that it was an artificial construct: that, if it referred to destructive processes in the group, it should be named thus rather than extracted as a separate concept; further, that it had connotations of the anti-Christ, which gave it a spurious and sinister association with evil. At the book launch of my first book on the anti-group, the same senior figure took me aside and asserted, "But I told you there was no such thing as the anti-group!"

My difficulty with these reactions was, and is, the extent to which the concept is concretised. In formulating the anti-group, I emphasised that it was first and foremost a critical principle, an attempt to give voice to a neglected aspect of groups, to provide a framework in which oppositional group processes could be understood. Only secondarily was it an explanatory concept, attempting to understand the aggression that groups could stimulate within and towards the group. Further, I emphasised throughout the creative potential of the anti-group, once recognised and addressed. However much I argued the case, the misunderstanding and misattribution persisted. I was accused of reifying a group process, yet felt that this was the reification of others. I remain confused. Were these valid concerns that I needed to take heed of, or did they reflect anger towards the rebel writer, me: anger that I dared to challenge the father, anger that I subverted my place in the generational hierarchy, and anger that I attracted recognition for a seemingly ill-conceived and destructive concept?

Reactions to my second book on desire and sexuality in the group (Nitsun, 2006) have been quieter but similarly ambivalent. In this case, positive and negative reactions seemed to be divided between countries. In the USA, a senior colleague endorsed it as "another classic in the field". The book was reviewed almost rapturously in an American group psychotherapy journal: a long, imaginative, and highly appreciative review, echoed in similar reviews in at least one or two other countries. By contrast, in the UK, the two reviews I read struck me as ungenerous, if not mean. I felt that they did scant justice to the book. Here again, I was nonplussed. Am I a prophet in my own land? The experience of not being appreciated in one's own community is not uncommon. But, once again, was my challenging the near-silence on the "dangerous" subject of sexuality and desire in the group too challenging to the *status quo*? Was the discomfort about sexuality openly explored in the group and in my book too great? This impression is reinforced by positive and appreciative reactions to the book in *non*-group analytic journals in the UK. Papers and books *outside* the group analytic community endorsed the book for its courage and usefulness.

I crave the reader's patience, if not indulgence, at this point. I am aware of trying to excise some of my own confusion, to use this opportunity to make sense of contradictions that are specific to me in a highly personal way. But I am also trying to tell the story of the rebel writer, which may touch on the fears and experiences of others who risk censure in what they write. In my experience, some of the fears are not ill-founded.

The creative–destructive dimension

Joyce Schlochower, in Chapter Two, quotes Aaron (1995), who suggests that psychoanalytic writers "must allow themselves to create a fantasy of recasting or even destroying the work of their analytic forefathers". Aaron suggests that fantasies of this sort are empowering and can augment creativity. This raises for me the very important link between creativity and destructiveness. It is not an unusual surmise that the two go hand in hand. Many artists have made similar statements. Picasso wrote: "Every act of creativity is also an act of destruction". As a painter myself, I can identify immediately with this thesis. I experience the act of painting as a constant movement between destructive and creative. The process involves a continuing process of creating an image, even a rudimentary mark, which is then destroyed to make way for another image or mark, and so on in a restless cycle that may or may not end up in a satisfactory new creation. Although this occurs at a gestural level, it also draws on the underlying tension between creative and destructive. This takes an even stronger form in writing where the antecedents are often clearer, in the form of the forefathers and the theories they have spawned that have become the law of the discipline.

The rebellious writer may be even more caught up than others in this spiral. In my own case, I have often wondered about my motives. Was my original challenge issued with destructive intent? How much was it an enactment of unresolved problems about authority, was group analysis a projection screen for attacks on my father, on my parents' generation? Is the irritable, critical response to my work a retributive act, an attempt to undermine me, to disempower my arguments? How much does envy play a part in the configuration? These questions highlight a dialectical process that has elements of both the depressive and paranoid-schizoid positions. Ultimately, I believe that my aims were not destructive but that I have enough valency for the depressive position to believe that perhaps I have been damaging, that I have hurt and offended, and that I deserve retribution, hence also expecting to be abandoned, if not annihilated, by those in authority in my field as well as by my peers. Exaggerated as this thinking may seem, I suggest that it is not unique to me and that the impulse to write and publish triggers the powerful anxieties of early development when the world held much creative promise but was also fraught with danger. The rebel writer, I suggest, embodies for both him/herself and others the rewards and risks of such a venture.

Conclusion

As writers in the psychotherapy field, we enter a complex world in which conformity and innovation exist in dialectical tension, in which our institutions live on a knife-edge between compliance and creativity. To position oneself as a writer in this environment is a daunting task, inviting recognition and risking rejection. The rebellious impulse conflicts with the longing to be appreciated and to belong. It invites counter-challenge, sometimes acrimonious, and the prospect of misunderstanding and misattribution. In taking this journey, however fraught, one comes face to face with oneself, with one's deepest issues about authority and the support of peers. While I have looked at these themes in a very personal way, I hope this is of value to others, perhaps those entering the minefield of publication and needing to prepare for the sometimes perplexing and unsettling range of potential reactions. At the same time, we mostly share a life-long quest for an authentic voice. Finding and sharing this voice with others in writing remains an unpredictable but usually affirming and life-enhancing means to this end.

Chapter 12

Raiding the inarticulate

The clinical case study and the representation of trauma

Maggie Turp

Entropy is described in Wikipedia as "measurement of the disorder or randomness of a system". In a closed system, entropy always moves in the direction of increasing disorder. It is not necessary to understand the laws of thermodynamics, of which entropy is the second, to observe this constant tendency towards disorder—and the substantial effort involved in bringing coherence, and thus meaning, to the "mess" of the wider world.

Different lines of work pursue the search for coherence in different ways. Scientists seek out pattern and order amid a complex maze of interacting variables by means of experimentation and measurement. Writers seek to impose order on the general messiness of lived experience by way of the written word. As Alain de Botton has noted: "The wider world will always be a mess. But around work, you can sometimes have a radically different kind of experience: you can get on top of a problem and finally resolve it. You can bring order to chaos for a bit" (De Botton, 2017).

T. S. Eliot in *Four Quartets* refers to the work of writing as a "raid on the inarticulate", a phrase that may resonate at a number of different levels with practitioners, for are our patients not engaged from the outset in their own "raid on the inarticulate" as they struggle to find the right words for the troubled and troubling experiences that have brought them to our door? As counsellors and psychotherapists, we stand beside them in this endeavour and actively participate via our careful listening and intermittent suggestions of suitable words and phrases. Those of us who choose also to write about our experiences engage with the same struggle at a higher level of abstraction, while at the same time striving to conserve in the written account something of the feel of the original encounter.

This chapter is about the art and science of psychotherapy writing, about the importance of case studies in our work and about the special challenges that arise in writing them. Because these challenges are multiplied in situations where a patient has been traumatised, the second half of the chapter has trauma as its focus. Trauma turns a person's life upside down: the door to chaos is thrown wide open. Furthermore, it is in the nature of trauma to resist representation. And yet writing about patients whose lives have been affected by trauma and representing their experience is part of process of understanding trauma and its aftermath and discovering how we might best help those who have suffered.

In all of my work, I have argued for the significance of the individual example and its key contribution to our understanding. Perhaps the most important expression of this argument has been the unusually large proportion of each publication I have accorded to "live" case study or infant observation examples. I have been able to do the same in this chapter thanks to the generosity of "Declan", a former patient who suffered a major traumatic loss at an early age and who has both given permission for and collaborated in the writing of a case study relating to his experience in psychotherapy.

The science and art of the case study

According to the poet Carlo Rovelli (2017), "Our culture is foolish to keep science and poetry separated: they are two tools to open our eyes to the complexity and beauty of the world." If the science of our work as psychotherapy writers is to impose order on the complexity that is a lived life, then the poetry of our work is to represent the subjective experience of those who come to us for help. Our task is, on the one hand, the discovery of regular patterns in the phenomena we witness and, on the other, the humanist endeavour shared with documentary and fiction writing—that of exploring and awakening compassion for the inner lives of others. Every case study is a raid on the inarticulate. A conversation between a practitioner and patient is as complex and messy as any other conversation. In addition, much of what transpires resides outside the domain of the verbal, in gestures, shifts of tone and volume, changes in posture and facial expression, pauses and silences and intakes of breath.

For the psychotherapy writer, the task is to be both scientist and artist and, as an artist, to have due regard for the particularity of every individual experience. As Philip Roth (1998) writes: "As an artist the nuance is your task. Your task is *not* to simplify. The task remains to impart the nuance, to elucidate the complication, to imply the contradiction."

Psychotherapy's way of engaging with the task of identifying pattern and order while at the same time allowing for nuance and contradiction is the case study. From Freud onwards, we have been engaged in a kind of dance between theory and practice. On the one hand, formulations of the possible ways in which the inner world of an individual may function—and at times malfunction—originate in and are refined by clinical experience. On the other, when we share our patients' stories with others, we re-clothe our theories with the experiences out of which they arose.

If theory is in essence orderly, then lived experience, including the experience of a fifty-minute therapy session, is anything but. In our clinical work, we set ourselves the task of finding meaning in what might initially seem random, rambling, and potentially meaningless. In case study writing, we seek to communicate not only our findings but also what we see, feel, and think as we engage in this task and as our relationship with a patient develops. When we do this well, it becomes possible for readers to "see" how the patient experiences his or her world. Readers have the option of making their own interpretations of the material presented, which may be different to the writer's interpretations. This is important not only for those of us who practise as therapists but also for a wider audience of non-professional readers. The nature, meaning, and consequences of emotional suffering are live themes in all of our lives, not just in the lives of patients and practitioners. It is through the case study that we most readily communicate, both with each other and with a wider audience of non-professional readers.

To do our job well, we need to think about behaviour in context and communicate the context to the reader. The importance of this dimension of understanding experience has been underlined in recent years by findings from the relatively new field of cognitive ethology. Researchers have demonstrated how a failure to take account of the *Umwelt* of the creature under observation can lead to fundamentally incorrect conclusions. In one example, De Waal (2016) narrates the evolving story of gibbon research. Gibbons were long considered to be less intelligent than chimpanzees and other monkeys because they performed poorly in tool-using tasks other primates could perform with ease. Even picking up a stick from the ground and using it to move a banana so that they could reach it seemed to be beyond them. De Waal's team noted that gibbons, unlike other primates, swing and hang in trees and rarely descend to ground level. Their hands, evolved for their arboreal life, lack a fully opposable thumb, with the result that picking up objects is very difficult for them. When the tests were re-designed to take account of the gibbons' specific adaptations to the world they inhabit, they performed just as well as other primate species and the myth of the foolish gibbon was dispelled. In similar vein, part of the endeavour of case study writing is to offer the reader the opportunity to witness the patient in his or her *Umwelt*, to offer the opportunity to vicariously enter into the patient's inner and outer world and make new and individual discoveries in relation to it.

The clinical case study and the patient's right to confidentiality

If we genuinely wish to convey a patient's subjective experience, we have to be specific: a general, overarching account will not do. For example, I could write, "A male patient, Ian, was emotionally and physically abused as a child by his mother." Or I could write, "A male patient, Ian, was the child of a single mother, who sometimes became enraged for no apparent reason. Ian tells me about a time when he asked his mother a question while she was watching television. She erupted in fury, chased him up the stairs and cornered him in his bedroom, where she gouged him with her finger-nails, *under my T-shirt where the teachers wouldn't see.*" Communication of the subjective experience of another person will always fall short of the full reality but a specific, detailed account can enable the reader to be with the writer and with the patient to a degree, as he or she seeks to tune in to the experiences being narrated in the consulting room.

At the same time, it is a central principle of psychotherapy that what transpires in the consulting room is confidential. We undertake not to write about a patient in a way that reveals his or her identity. A recent event and ensuing correspondence underlined the contested nature of the case study and the snares and pitfalls that are strewn across the path of any practitioner who chooses to write about a patient. It began with an allegation that a practitioner, Loftus, had violated the right to confiden-tiality of a subject of a case history. The allegation was debated in 2014 via a series of publications in the *Journal of Interpersonal Violence*.[1] In a letter published in *The Psychologist* in February 2017, Ashley Conway writes that "Loftus's actions in this case have now made it ethically prob-lematic for any psychology journal to publish case histories".

The problem, then, is a serious one for all of us who wish to com-municate our experience of clinical work via case study accounts. One possible solution takes the form of a "mix and match" combination of elements from the narratives of several patients. With a modicum of nar-rative smoothing, these can be combined in a single case study. I have taken this approach myself on occasion, including in my first book,[2] but it is by no means foolproof. I recently presented a composite case study at a conference, only to have it identified by one of the delegates, an ex-patient, as his personal story. The ex-patient stood up and asserted to the full lecture hall that this was *his* story, that I was talking about him and moreover using his story *without permission*. Fortunately, he was willing to meet with me subsequently, giving me the opportunity to hear him out, apologise for the distress I had inadvertently caused, and explain that the case study was in fact a composite. By way of illustration, I was able to point to various details that could not have applied to him. However, although the differences were there, I was also able to understand why he had genuinely thought I was talking about him and him alone: in his position, I might well have come to the same conclusion.

Since this occurrence, I have become more wary of composite case studies. It is part of our human nature to identify our own stories in the stories of others. Indeed, I have read that medical students, as they work their way through texts describing the many different ways in which the body can succumb to disease, experience each "disease of the week" in turn. Who is to say that the same will not apply to patients and ex-patients in psychotherapy?

If we are unhappy about composites, another option is to create fictions. In *The Impossibility of Sex*, Susie Orbach (1996) states openly that the case examples in the book are made up. I have enjoyed a lifelong love affair with novels, films, and plays and, in common with the editor of this book Martin Weegmann,[3] I have learned at least as much about human nature and its vicissitudes from fiction as from psychotherapy texts. There is much to appreciate in Orbach's refreshingly forthright approach. However—perhaps on account of my social science background—I find myself uncomfortable with the idea of inventing case studies and presenting them as "evidence" of the arguments being advanced. Case studies are our major source of empirical data, the equivalent of the raw data provided in scientific journals in the form of tables of results. Without raw data, the reader is not in a position to form his or her opinion as to whether the results have been correctly interpreted. We are trying to learn from each other's work—from our failures as well as our successes—and the most obvious and helpful resources for learning are the actual situations and narratives our patients bring to us. How much confidence can we have in the wider conclusions drawn in a book or journal paper when the material upon which the conclusions are based is entirely fictitious?

A third alternative is to ask the patient for permission to publish, and this is the path I now follow whenever possible. If I feel able to ask for permission and the patient agrees, I discuss with the patient that fact that he or she is likely to recognise himself or herself in the story, although all details that might identify him or her to a third party will be changed. I also offer the patient the option of reading the text prior to publication and suggesting amendments or requesting the exclusion of details they feel might be identifying. While this may be (and in my view is) a "gold standard" approach, it is important to acknowledge that it is by no means a perfect solution. Like everything the practitioner says and does, a request for permission to publish falls into the context of the patient's previous experience, both in life and in therapy. There are situations—for example, where a patient's past experience has been marked by over-exposure and shaming—where a request for permission to publish risks undermining the work that has been done in therapy and must therefore be avoided.

The representation of trauma

When a patient has been traumatised, as is the case with many of the people who seek our help, the raid on the inarticulate takes on an additional dimension. We are confronted not only with the difficulties and complications outlined above but also with the additional difficulty of representing what can never fully represented on account of its traumatic "beyond words" nature. Indeed, it is in the essence of trauma that it is *not* represented and remembered in the usual storied and ordered way characteristic of non-traumatic events. The traumatising incident or situation resides in the brain in snapshots and sounds and smells that invade the consciousness of the traumatised person at will; the experience is not so much of remembering as of being haunted. Things that have happened in the past rear up in the mind of the sufferer as though they are happening again, right here and right now and with the full force of the original horror.

If it is science—in this case neuroscience—that has furnished us with an account of the brain processes in play, it is in the domain of the arts that many attempts at representation reside. In a lecture in 2016, the psychoanalyst Gregorio Kohon showed slides of Amish Kapoor's attempt to represent the trauma of the Holocaust in the form of a sculpture located in Jerusalem. The sculpture, a huge mushroom-shaped structure made of metal with shiny, reflective surfaces, turns the world upside down and back to front for those who walk beneath and around it. Familiar reference points are rendered unfamiliar: it is hard to know which way you are facing or how to orient yourself in the strange and distorted world the sculpture creates.

Amish Kapoor's sculpture will have different associations and meanings for different viewers—something that is also true of those who read our written communications in journal papers and books. The reader looks to us on the one hand to impose order, to offer, if you like, a "reading" of the situation and, on the other hand, to communicate something of the essence of what it is like for a particular patient to be in a particular mental space and world of experience at a particular time. When we are able to successfully blend these two elements, we offer the reader the opportunity to register his or her own impressions and arrive at his or her own understandings. The material we have to work with is not metal or paint or clay or stone but language. In his written work, Kohon (2016) reflects in depth on the nature of aesthetic experience and the way in which the reader/viewer engages with the artist to create meaning. Our work has a practical and professionally specific aim—to learn from our own experience and that of others and thereby increase our understanding of mental distress and how it might be ameliorated—but the aesthetic nature of the communication remains important. George Orwell also characterised his work as having a practical and specific aim, the explicit aim of exposing and combatting totalitarianism. Nevertheless, in *Why I Write*, he emphasised that *any* piece of writing, whether a book, newspaper report, or magazine article, must constitute an "aesthetic experience" if it is to have any effect (Owell, 1946).

The traumatised patient and the clinical case study

The question of confidentiality can be a source of additional complications where a patient has been subject to traumatic events or situations of an unusual and highly specific nature. Some traumas affect large numbers of people and the complication does not then arise. For example, in *Understanding Trauma* Caroline Garland (1998) describes her work with a twelve-year-old boy who had been caught up in the catastrophic events at Hillsborough football stadium in 1989. Because there would have been many boys of that age at the match on that fateful day, the trauma the boy suffered is not highly identifying and no particular difficulties arise in relation to confidentiality.

Some traumas, however, are highly specific: what has happened to the patient in question involves such an unlikely combination of elements that is almost certainly unique. When this is the case, the need to protect confidentiality necessitates a degree of fictionalisation. Furthermore, the details that need to be fictionalised—namely, the exact nature and circumstances of the trauma—are those at the very heart of the patient's story. The task is to communicate the emotional truth of the trauma without offering a factual account of what happened. When this situation arises, as it did with the patient I have called "Declan", I found my mind awash with questions. Which identifying details could simply be omitted without the essence of the trauma becoming lost? Which would need to be replaced with invented details? What kind of scenario could I come up with that would carry the same emotional weight as the original event? These considerations were additional to those that always need to be considered, in particular the need to communicate the tenor of the therapeutic relationship and the tone of the work. After all, the point is not so much to tell the patient's story as to show a way of working, to invite the reader into a scene of "therapy in action".

Declan undertook a period of psychotherapy within the last two years. He has both given permission for this account to be written and published and collaborated in the writing of his own story. Our patients come to us for help, they pay our fees, and when they leave they owe us nothing. To be offered such generous help is a genuinely moving experience. What follows in the final section of the chapter is an account both of the work itself and the process of writing about the work.

Declan's story

As will emerge, Declan was involved in a traumatic accident as a young boy. The accident was reported in the local press and it was not unusual in the years that followed for someone who had read the report, for example Declan's piano teacher, to make the link to Declan and bring it up in conversation. Since a factual description of the trauma would be likely to identify Declan not only to family and friends but also to anyone who had read the newspaper report, it was evident from the start that the details of the trauma would have to be changed. One of the challenges of writing this particular case study was therefore to come up with a scenario with the potential to re-create in the reader something of the patient's response to what happened.

My understanding of his response was based to some extent on my own response to his description of the traumatic incident. I remember how my eyes opened wide in disbelief when Declan described the sequence of events and how my mind went over and over the single pointless question: "How could such a thing happen?" I have been relieved of some responsibility in relation to the question of whether or not my substituted account is on the one hand emotionally accurate and on the other non-identifying by Declan's generous offer to collaborate in the writing.

As well as attempting to represent the trauma, I have been engaged with the usual questions that arise when writing a case study. What to include and what to leave out? How to sequence the material? Whether to narrate the patient's story in its original, chronological order or in the order in which things emerged in psychotherapy? The first option allows the reader to easily follow the course of events while the second has the advantage of inviting him or her into the consulting room to witness and think about what transpires. In a not unusual compromise between coherence and verisimilitude, I find myself opting for a combination of the two, beginning the case study with an account of Declan's intimate relationships, which is where Declan himself began.

One of the first things Declan tells me was that he has previously been in analysis for some years. He has found it helpful in many ways but he still suffers from crippling episodes of depression. These have been so severe and disabling that he has had to return to his family home on a number of occasions to be looked after. On one occasion, he had to leave his job in a foreign country and fly home. I hear the frustration in his voice when he tells me about these incidents.

Declan has a good understanding of what triggers his depressive episodes, perhaps as a consequence of his time in analysis. It is always the same thing: becoming involved in a new love relationship. As things become more serious and the emotional tie strengthens, Declan becomes preoccupied with the fear of losing his own feeling of love for the new love in his life, in fact for losing all feeling and becoming numb, as has happened in the past. He becomes overwhelmed by a state of anticipatory sadness and breaks down. He is then obliged to return home in order to recover and this brings the relationship to an end.

I ask Declan to tell me about his various relationships, and it emerges that they include a marriage that lasted six years. I note that Declan must have managed to navigate the torments of the initial stages of the relationship on that one occasion and ask him if he has any idea what was different that time round. Several conversations later, the answer is clear. Declan loved his wife but the relationship was devoid of sexual passion, primarily because his wife was continually averse to having sexual relations with him. They occasionally had sex but he always felt he was imposing himself upon her against his will, which left him feeling guilty and ashamed. He found an outlet for his frustrated sexual desires in pornography, which further increased his sense of shame. An aspect of the story that really surprised me was that Declan stayed in the marriage for as long as he did, and might indeed have stayed longer had his wife not told him, six years in, that she did not ever want to have children. In relation to the divorce, Declan tells me that he has "let everyone down".

New love relationships bring with them a great deal of anxiety as well as hope. To allow oneself to become emotionally involved is to take a risk. Nothing is certain in the early stages of the affair and a painful loss is something that most of us have probably feared or experienced at one time or another. However, most of us do not break down. Why is the fear of loss so disabling for Declan that he is unable to carry on? Declan tells me he knows from his analysis that the answer must be linked to the sudden death of his father when he was only three years old. What he cannot understand is the why and the how.

I ask Declan to tell me about his father dying. The family was travelling with his family in their car when a piece of masonry fell from a bridge that was in the process of being renovated. It came down through the windscreen and hit Declan's father on the head. His father died at the wheel. Nobody else in the family was injured. Declan's mother managed to take control of the steering wheel and bring the car to a halt at the side of the road. Declan has a screen memory of the event and is able to draw for me the vehicles as he saw them after the accident, including the police car and the fire engine, and himself standing in the road screaming.

The community where the family lived was close-knit and the extended family rallied around. A striking feature of the situation was that way in which Declan's father "disappeared". Nobody really spoke about him. There were no photographs of him on the wall. His birthday was not remembered. Declan remembers hearing his mother crying in her room and knowing not to upset her more by talking about his father. Two years on, Declan's mother remarried and the silence deepened. Declan's sense at this point was that mentioning his father would remind his stepfather that he hadn't been the first love in his mother's life. It would have been too awkward, too embarrassing.

Declan tells me his stepfather is a wonderful man who has always been loving and supportive. However, he finds it hard to understand Declan's depressions. And what, Declan asks me, has he got to be depressed about? He has a lovely family and a good job. He has been lucky, luckier than most. Yes, he has let everyone down! By the time he was Declan's age, his father was married with children, a responsible family man. And what has he done? At work, he doesn't always work that hard. Sometimes he looks at stuff on the internet when he is supposed to be working. "I'm a waste of space", he tells me. I ask him if he would speak to anyone else the way he speaks to himself. He smiles ruefully and says, "I wouldn't speak to my dog like that!" I say that if someone spoke to me the way Declan speaks to himself, I would probably be depressed too. I ask him to try to notice all the times in the week when he speaks disparagingly to himself and tell me about them at our next appointment.

Later in the therapy, Declan tells me about a time in secondary school when he traded on his "fame" to make himself seem interesting and attractive to potential girlfriends, a memory that has left him feeling deeply ashamed. I say that I understand how mortifying it must be for him to remember behaviour he finds so shameful. At the same time, when something like the trauma he went through occurs, the traces do not simply disappear. The people closest to Declan, those who could in principle have helped him to mourn his loss, were themselves too traumatised to do so. He was left with no outlet for his feelings and no idea what to do with them. With this in mind, it is perhaps it was not entirely surprising that the traces of the trauma found their way to the surface in strange, even perverse, ways.

We talk a lot about Declan's memories of his father. Declan loved and admired him with all the intensity that a three-year-old boy can bring to a relationship with a father who loves him in return. At the time of the therapy, I have a three-year-old grandson who similarly adores his father. I ask myself what it would be like for him to lose his beloved Dad. I do not stay with the question for long: the feelings are too hard to bear. The sessions with Declan become the context for the process of re-membering, regressing, re-imagining, and grieving. Towards the end of therapy, Declan remembers some of the ways in which his father wasn't perfect. For example, he had a fling with another woman—or so it was said—when he was already engaged! I am happy to witness Declan's idealisation of his father abating. Declan no longer has to compare himself with somebody perfect, somebody he could never live up to. His relentless attacks on himself for the ways in which he is less than perfect are less in evidence now. He is finally growing into the person he is, rather than identifying himself as a lesser version of his father.

Around this time, Declan becomes involved with another woman. This time round, I am there for him to talk through the fantasies and fears that come to the fore as the relationship deepens. On one occasion, Declan tells me he put his hand on her arm at a certain point during a movie and *she did not put her hand on top of his.* This, he is sure, means that she is cooling towards him. The fear that this might be the case is inexorably linked with the primary fear that torments him, the sudden disappearance of his own loving feelings towards her. I wonder how I might figuratively put my hand on top of Declan's hand at this critically wobbly moment. The reassurance I am able to give is that his fears, and fears of his fears, by no means disqualify him from sustaining a loving relationship. I introduce the idea that he might usefully let his girlfriend know about his fears and some of the understandings we have reached about the events that underpin them. I suggest that she may even have some fears of her own.

Declan does decide to take the risk of talking directly with his girl-friend about the trauma and its aftermath, in particular the intense anx-iety stirred up in him by small incidents that feel rejecting, even when he knows rationally that they are not. To his profound relief, she is im-mensely loving and reassuring. The relationship moves forward. He takes her to visit his family and is thrilled when they confirm his high opinion of her. On a subsequent family visit, she asks them about Declan's birth father and says she would be interested to see some photos—something Declan himself has felt unable to do. Photos are produced. Declan takes some home with him, frames them, and puts them up on the wall.

This was never intended to be a long therapy and we are both start-ing to think that the time to end is approaching. The week that Declan comes in and joyfully announces his intention to propose to his new love, we make the decision. We set the date, leaving a few weeks to review our work and make the ending. Declan asks whether he can contact me again if he finds himself in trouble. I say that he can and ask him how likely he thinks it is that he will become depressed again. He seems surprised, as well as relieved, to find himself saying that he thinks he will be fine.

This, then, is the story of the story and the writing of the story, the particular blend of fact and fiction characteristic of a case study written for publication. There was an accident. A father died. It is faction, in the sense of being a blend of fact and fiction and in the sense also of being "factional". This is the way I remember the sessions, *my* version—edited down and smoothed over. If Declan wrote the account, it would be dif-ferent, although I hope not unrecognisably so. And it is partly fiction, drawn from my imagination and imbued as far as my capabilities allow, with the emotion and spirit of the events narrated by the patient.

I am leaving the final word to Declan. The concluding paragraphs are taken from the email he sent in response to my request for permission to write about our work together.

Dear Maggie,

Great to hear from you and thank you for getting in touch.

The work I did with you was invaluable as it gave me a huge opportunity to really consider the traumatic events that happened and how they were affecting me later in life. Although I do get reoccurrence of the depressive episodes, I am able to look at the situation holistically and "cut myself some slack", so to speak. The main trigger if you remember was loving relationships, and I have found the love of my life (whom I married in November) so with this comes certain emotional caveats which I know I must learn to live with.

I would be happy and honoured for you to write about it. Regarding the events, it happened in X a long time ago and was covered by one small article in the X Times in 1982. The actual details of the accident could be reinvented but I guess there should be similarities in so far as the only person who was harmed in the accident was my father. So my Mum, Aunt, brother and I witnessed the event as back seat passengers without the physical trauma of a car crash for example, where everyone would have been injured. I think this is an important aspect to convey.

Hysterically crying uninjured after the accident is one memory that will be with me forever.

Note

1 See Dalenberg, C. J. (2014). Protecting scientists, science and case protagonists: a discussion of Taus v. Loftus commentaries. *Journal of Interpersonal Violence, 9*: 3308–3234; Kluemper, N. S. (2014). Published case reports: one woman's account of having her confidentiality violated. *Journal of Interpersonal Violence, 29*: 3232–3234; and Olafson, E. (2014). A review and correction of the errors in Loftus and Gruyer on Jane Doe, *Journal of Interpersonal Violence, 29*: 3245–3259.

References

Abbasi, A. (2012). A very dangerous conversation: the patient's internal conflicts elaborated through the use of ethnic and religious differences between patient and analyst. *International Journal of Psycho-Analysis, 93*: 515–534.

Abraham, K. (1924). A short study of the development of the libido, viewed in the light of the mental disorders. In: *Selected Papers of Karl Abraham*, trans. D. Bryan & A. Strachey. London: Hogarth, 1973.

Arendt, H. (1958). *The Human Condition.* Chicago: University of Chicago Press.

Aron, L. (1995). The internalized primal scene. *Psychoanalytic Dialogues, 5*: 195–223.

Barratt, B. *(2013) What is Psychoanalysis: 100 Years after Freud's Secret Committee.* London: Routledge.

Barthes, R. (1977). From work to text. In: *Image, Music, Text*, trans. S. Heath. London: Fontana Press.

Barwick, N. (1995). Pandora's Box: an investigation of essay anxiety in adolescents. *Psychodynamic Counselling, 1*(4): 560–575.

Barwick, N. (2000). Loss, creativity and leaving home: investigating adolescent essay anxiety. In: N. Barwick (Ed.), *Clinical Counselling in Schools.* London: Routledge.

Benveniste, D. (2015). *The Interwoven Lives of Sigmund, Anna and W. Ernest Freud: Three Generations of Psychoanalysis.* New York: The American Institute for Psychoanalysis.

Bion, W. R. (1962a). *Learning from Experience.* London: Heinemann.

Bion, W. R. (1962b). A theory of thinking. In: *Second Thoughts.* London: Karnac, 1984.

Bloom, H. (1973). *The Anxiety of Influence.* Oxford: Oxford University Press.

Bloom, H. (1997). *The Anxiety of Influence: A Theory of Poetry.* Oxford: Oxford University Press.

Bloom, H. (2011). *The Anatomy of Influence: Literature as a Way of Life.* New York: Yale University Press.

Bollas, C. (1987). *The Shadow of the Object.* New York: Columbia University Press.

Bollas, C. (1994). *Being a Character: Psychoanalysis and Self Experience.* New York: Hill & Wang.

Bollas, C. (1997). *Cracking Up: The Work of Unconscious Experience.* London: Routledge.

Boyarin, D. (1997). *Unheroic Conduct: The Rise of Heterosexuality and the Invention of the Jewish Man*. Berkeley: University of California Press.

Brande, D. (1996). *Becoming a Writer*. London: Macmillan.

Britton, R. (1985). The Oedipus situation and the depressive position. In: *Clinical Lectures on Klein and Bion*. London: Routledge, 1992.

Britton, R. (1989). The missing link: parental sexuality in the Oedipus complex. In: R. Britton, M. Feldman, & E. O'Shaughnessy, *The Oedipus Complex Today*. London: Karnac.

Britton, R. (1997). Making the private public. In: I. Ward (Ed.), *The Presentation of Case Material in Clinical Discourse*. London: Karnac.

Britton, R. (1998). Daydream, phantasy and fiction. In: *Belief and Imagination: Explorations in Psychoanalysis* (pp. 109–119). Hove and New York: Brunner Routledge.

Britton, R. (2003). The preacher, the poet and the psychoanalyst. In: H. Canham & C. Satyamurti (Eds.), *Acquainted with the Night: Psychoanalysis and the Poetic Imagination* (pp. 113–132). London: Karnac.

Bruner, J. (1994). The "Remembered Self". In: U. Neisser & R. Fivush (Eds.), *The Remembering Self: Construction and Accuracy in the Self-Narrative* (Chapter 2). Boston: Cambridge University Press.

Buckley, J., Hedge, A., Yates, T., et al. (2015). The sedentary office: a growing case for change towards better health and productivity. *British Journal of Sports Medicine*. http://dx.doi.org/10.1136/bjsports-2015-094618

Carson, D., & Becker, K. (2003). *Creativity in Therapy*. London: Routledge.

Chabert, C. (2012). The analyst at work: a review of *A Very Dangerous Conversation* by Aisha Abbasi. *International Journal of Psychoanalysis*, *93*: 545–554.

Chinua, A. (1958). *Things Fall Apart*. London: Everyman's Library, 2010.

Coleridge, S. (1817). *Biographia Literaria*. London: Book Jungle, 2008.

Critchley, S. (2004). *Very Little... Almost Nothing: Death, Philosophy and Literature*. London: Routledge.

Dalenberg, C. J. (2014). Protecting scientists, science and case protagonists: a discussion of Taus v. Loftus commentaries. *Journal of Interpersonal Violence, 9*: 3308–3234.

De Botton, A. (2017). My working day. *The Guardian*, 28 January.

De Posadas, L. (2012). A commentary on *A Very Dangerous Conversation* by Aisha Abbasi. *International Journal of Psycho-Analysis*, *93*: 535–544.

De Waal, F. (2016). *Are We Smart Enough to Know How Smart Animals Are?* London: Granta.

Derrida, J. (1967). Structure, sign and play in the discourse of human sciences. In: *Writing and Difference*, trans. A. Bass. Chicago: University of Chicago Press.

Dews, P. (1987). *Logics of Disintegration: Post-Structuralist Thought and the Claims of Critical Theory*. New York: Verso.

Eliot, T. S. (1922). The Wasteland. In: *The Complete Poems and Plays*. London: Faber and Faber, 1978.

Eliot, T. S. (1954). East Coker. In: *Four Quartets*. London: Faber and Faber.

Epston, D. (1994). Extending the conversation. *Family Therapy Networker*, 18(6): pp. 31–37, 62–63.

Feldman, R. (2015). *Child Development*. London: Pearson Education.

Fischer, R. (2003). *A History of Writing*. London: Reaktion Books.

Fonagy, P., Gergely, G., Jurist, E. L., & Target, M. (2002). *Affect Regulation, Mentalization and the Development of the Self.* New York: Other Press.

Foster Wallace, D. (2012). *Both Flesh and Not.* London: Little, Brown and Company.

Foster Wallace, D., & Garner, B. A. (2013). *Quack this Way.* London: Penrose.

Foucault, M. (1977). *Language, Counter-Memory, Practice: Selected Essays and Interviews*, Ed. and Trans. D. Bouchard. Ithaca: Cornell University Press.

Foulkes, S. H. (1964). *Therapeutic Group Analysis.* London: Allen and Unwin. [Reprinted, London: Karnac, 1986.]

Freud, S. (1905d). Three Essays on the Theory of Sexuality. *The Standard Edition of the Complete Psychological Works of Sigmund Freud, 7.* London: Hogarth.

Freud, S. (1905e). Fragment of an analysis of a case of hysteria. *The Standard Edition of the Complete Psychological Works of Sigmund Freud, 7.* London: Hogarth.

Freud, S. (1908e). Creative writers and day-dreaming. *The Standard Edition of the Complete Psychological Works of Sigmund Freud, 9.* London: Hogarth.

Freud, S. (1909b). Analysis of a phobia in a five-year-old boy. *The Standard Edition of the Complete Psychological Works of Sigmund Freud, 10.* London: Hogarth.

Freud, S. (1909d). Notes upon a case of obsessional neurosis. *The Standard Edition of the Complete Psychological Works of Sigmund Freud, 10.* London: Hogarth.

Freud, S. (1911c). Psycho-analytic notes on an autobiographical account of a case of paranoia. *The Standard Edition of the Complete Psychological Works of Sigmund Freud, 12.* London: Hogarth.

Freud, S. (1912) Recommendations to Physicians Practising Psycho-Analysis. *The Standard Edition of the Complete Psychological Works of Sigmund Freud, 12.* London: Hogarth.

Freud, S. (1916e). Introductory Lectures on Psychoanalysis. *The Standard Edition of the Complete Psychological Works of Sigmund Freud, 16.* London: Hogarth.

Freud, S. (1917e). Mourning and melancholia. *The Standard Edition of the Complete Psychological Works of Sigmund Freud, 17.* London: Hogarth.

Freud, S. (1920g). Beyond the Pleasure Principle. *The Standard Edition of the Complete Psychological Works of Sigmund Freud, 18.* London: Hogarth.

Freud, S. (1930a). Civilization and its Discontents. *The Standard Edition of the Complete Psychological Works of Sigmund Freud, 21.* London: Hogarth.

Frosh, S. (2017). Different trains: an essay in memorialising. *American Imago, 74,* 1–22.

Frye, N. (1957). *Anatomy of Criticism: Four Essays.* New Jersey: Princeton University Press.

Garland, C. (Ed.) (1998). *Understanding Trauma: A Psychoanalytic Approach.* London: Duckworth.

Gee, M. (1988). Seminar on novel writing, MA in Language, the Arts, and Education. University of Sussex.

Goodall, H. (2001). *Big Bangs: The Story of Five Discoveries that Changed Musical History.* London: Vintage.

Gordon, M. (2001). Putting pen to paper, but not just any pen to just any paper. In: *Writers on Writing: Collected Essays from The New York Times.* New York: Henry Holt & Co.

146   References

Green, A. (1975). The analyst, symbolization and absence in the analytic setting (On changes on analytic practice and analytic experience)—In memory of D. W. Winnicott. *International Journal of Psycho-Analysis, 56*: 1–22.

Greenacre, P. (1957). The childhood of the artist: libidinal phase development and giftedness. *Psychoanalytic Study of the Child, 12*: 47–72.

Grunebaum, A. (1984). *The Foundations of Psychoanalysis: A Philosophical Critique*. Berkeley: University of California Press.

Heimann, P. (1950). On counter-transference. *International Journal of Psycho-Analysis, 30*: 81–84.

Hobson, P. (2002). *The Cradle of Thought: Challenging the Origins of Thinking*. London: Macmillan.

Hoffman, E. (1989). *Lost in Translation: A Life in a New Language*. London: Heinemann.

Holmes, J. (2010). *Exploring in Security*. London: Routledge.

Holmes, J. (2014). *The Therapeutic Imagination*. London: Routledge.

Holmes, J., & Slade, A. (2017). *Attachment for Therapists: Science and Practice*. London: SAGE.

Holmes, R. (1999). *Coleridge: Darker Reflections*. London: Flamingo.

Joseph, B. (1978). Different types of anxiety and their handling in the analytic situation. *International Journal of Psycho-Analysis, 59*: 223–228.

Joyce, J. (1918). *Poems and Exiles*. London: Penguin, 2002.

Joyce, J. (1922/1960). *Ulysses*. London: Faber.

Keats, J. (2005). In: D. Wu (Ed.), *Romanticism: An Anthology* (third edition; p. 1351). Oxford: Blackwell.

Kernberg, O. (2003). The management of affect storms in the psychoanalytic psychotherapy of borderline patients. *Journal of the American Psychoanalytic Association, 51*: 517–544.

King James Authorised Version, *The Holy Bible*. Oxford: Oxford University Press.

Klein, M. (1932). *The Psychoanalysis of Children: The Writings of Melanie Klein, Volume 2*. London: Hogarth.

Klein, M. (1935). A contribution to the psychogenesis of manic-depressive states. In: *Love, Guilt and Reparation, and Other Works, 1921–1945*. London: Virago, 1988.

Klein, M. (1940). Mourning and its relation to manic-depressive states. In: *Love, Guilt and Reparation, and Other Works, 1921–1945*. London: Virago, 1988.

Klein, M. (1961). *Narrative of a Child Analysis*. London: Hogarth.

Kluemper, N. S. (2014). Published case reports: one woman's account of having her confidentiality violated. *Journal of Interpersonal Violence, 29*: 3232–3234.

Kohon, G. (2015). *Psychoanalysis and the Uncanny*. London: Routledge.

Kohon, G. (2016). *Reflections on the Aesthetic Experience*. Abingdon: Routledge.

Lacan, J. (1966). Seminar on "The Purloined Letter". In: J. Lacan, *Écrits*, Trans. B. Fink. New York: W. W. Norton, 2006.

Laland, K. (2017). *Darwin's Unfinished Symphony*. Princeton, NJ: Princeton University Press.

Laman, B. (2004). *James Joyce and German Theory*. Madison, NJ: Dickinson University Press.

Laplanche, J. (1999a). The unfinished Copernican revolution. In: J. Laplanche, *Essays on Otherness*. London: Routledge.

Laplanche, J. (1999b). Time and the Other. In: J. Laplanche & J. Fletcher, *Essays on Otherness* (p. 260). London: Routledge.

Leask, P. (2013a). Losing trust in the world: humiliation and its consequences. *Psychodynamic Practice, 19(2)*: 129–142.

Leask, P. (2013b). Humiliation as a weapon within the Party: fictional and personal accounts. In: M. Fulbrook & A. I. Port (Eds.), *Becoming East German: Socialist Structures and Sensibilities after Hitler.* New York and Oxford: Berghahn.

Levinas, E. (1987). *Time and the Other.* Trans. R. A. Cohen. Pittsburgh, PA: Duquesne University Press.

MacIntyre, A. (1984). *After Virtue: A Study in Moral Theory.* Indiana: University of Notre Dame Press.

Mahoney, P. (1989). *On Defining Freud's Discourse.* New Haven and London: Yale University Press.

Malan, D. (1979). *Individual Psychotherapy and the Science of Psychodynamics.* London: Butterworths.

McGilchrist, I. (2009). *The Master and His Emissary.* New Haven: Yale University Press.

McLuhan, M. (1964). *Understanding Media: The Extensions of Man.* Cambridge, MA: MIT Press, 1994.

Mears, R. (2005). *The Metaphor of Play.* London: Routledge.

Mendelsohn, D. (2010). But enough about me—what does the popularity of memoirs tell us about ourselves? *The New Yorker*, 25 January, p. 68.

Miller, I. S. (2015). *Defining Psychoanalysis.* London: Karnac.

Miller, I. S. (2016). *On Minding and Being Minded.* London: Karnac.

Miller, I. S., & Sweet, A. D. (2017). Psychic rigidity, therapeutic response and time: black holes, white holes, "D" and "d". *International Forum of Psychoanalysis, 26(2)*:97–104.

Miller, I. S., & Sweet, A. D. (2018). *On the Daily Work of Psychodynamic Psychotherapy.* London: Karnac.

Money-Kyrle, R. (1968). On cognitive development. *International Journal of Psycho-Analysis, 49*: 691–698.

Moskowitz, C. (1999). *Wyoming Trail.* London: Granta.

Nabokov, V. (1967). *Memory: an autobiography revisited.* London: Weidenfeld and Nicolson.

Nitsun, M. (1991). The anti-group: destructive forces in the group and their therapeutic potential. *Group Analysis, 24*: 7–20.

Nitsun, M. (1996). *The Anti-Group: Destructive Forces in the Group and Their Creative Potential.* London: Routledge.

Nitsun, M. (2006). *The Group as an Object of Desire: Sexuality in Group Psychotherapy.* London: Routledge.

Nitsun, M. (2009). Authority and revolt: the challenges to group leadership. *Group Analysis, 42*: 1–23.

Nitsun, M. (2015a). Rebel without a cause: authority and revolt as themes in the cinema. In: *Beyond the Anti-Group: Survival and Transformation.* London: Routledge.

Nitsun, M. (2015b). *Beyond the Anti-Group: Survival and Transformation.* London: Routledge.

Ogden, T. (1994). *Subjects of Analysis.* London: Karnac.

Ogden, T. (1997). *Reverie and Interpretation.* Northville, NJ: Jason Aronson.

Ogden, T. (2005). On psychoanalytic writing. *International Journal of Psycho-Analysis, 86*: 15–29.

Olafson, E. (2014). A review and correction of the errors in Loftus and Gruyer on Jane Doe. *Journal of Interpersonal Violence, 29*: 3245–3259.

Ondaatje, M. (2000). *Anil's Ghost*. London: Bloomsbury.

O'Neill, E. (1921). *Anna Christie, The Emperor Jones, The Hairy Ape*. Dover: Thrift Editions, 1995.

Orbach, S. (1996). *The Impossibility of Sex*. London: Simon and Schuster.

Orwell, G. (1946). *Why I Write*. London: Penguin Books.

Parker, C. (1995). *The Maybe*. Installation at the Serpentine Gallery, London, a collaboration between Cornelia Parker and Tilda Swinton.

Phillips, A. (1994). The shock of the old. *London Review of Books, 16(3)*.

Phillips, A. (1994). The telling of selves: notes on psychoanalysis and autobiography. In: *On Flirtation*. Harvard: Harvard University Press.

Phillips, A. (2006). *The Penguin Freud Reader*. London: Penguin Books.

Pontalis, J.-B. (1993). *Love of Beginnings*. Trans. J. Greene & M.-C. Regius. London: Free Association Books.

Raphael-Leff, J. (2010). The "Dreamer" by daylight: imaginative play, creativity, and generative identity. *Psychoanalytic Study of the Child, 64*: 14–53.

Raphael-Leff, J. (2015). *Dark Side of the Womb*. London: Anna Freud Centre.

Riviere, J. (1936). On the genesis of psychical conflict in earliest infancy. *International Journal of Psycho-Analysis, 17*: 395–422.

Roazen, P. (1969). *Brother Animal: The Story of Freud and Tausk*. New York: Knopf.

Roth, P. (1998). *I Married a Communist*. New York: Jonathan Cape.

Rovelli, C. (2017). *Reality Is Not What It Seems*. Trans. S. Carnell & E. Segre. London: Penguin.

Ruskin, J. (1856). *Selected Writings*, Ed. K. Clark. London: Penguin, 1964.

Russel, B. 1959. *My Philosophical Development*. London: George Allen & Unwin; New York: Simon & Schuster.

Rustin, M. (2001). *Reason and Unreason*. London: Continuum.

Rycroft, C. (1979). *The Innocence of Dreams*. London: Chatto.

Rycroft, C. (1985). *Psychoanalysis and Beyond*. London: Chatto.

Satre, J.-P. (1950). *What is Literature?* London: Methuen & Co. Ltd.

Schlapobersky, J. (2016). *From the Couch to the Circle: Group-Analytic Psychotherapy in Practice*. London: Routledge.

Schoen, D. (1991). *The Reflective Practitioner: How Professionals Think in Action*. Farnham: Ashgate.

Segal, H. (1989). Introduction. In: R. Britton, M. Feldman, & E. O'Shaughnessy, *The Oedipus Complex Today*. London: Karnac.

Segal, H. (1991). Imagination, play and art. In: *Dream, Phantasy and Art* (pp. 101–109). Hove, New York: Brunner Routledge.

Sharpe, E. (1940). Psycho-physical problems revealed in language: an examination of metaphor. *International Journal of Psycho-Analysis, 21*: 201–213.

Slessor, K. (1957). "Sleep". In: *Poems by Kenneth Slessor*. Sydney: Angus and Robertson.

Slochower, J. (1996). *Holding and Psychoanalysis: A Relational Perspective*. Hillsdale, NJ: The Analytic Press, 2014.

Slochower, J. (1996a). The holding environment and the fate of the analyst's subjectivity. *Psychoanalytic Dialogues, 6*: 323–353.

Slochower, J. (2006). *Psychoanalytic Collisions*. Hillsdale, NJ: The Analytic Press, 2014.

Sontag, S. (2001). Directions: write, read, rewrite. Repeat steps 2 and 3 as needed. *Writers on Writing: Collected Essays from the New York Times* (pp. 223–229). New York: New York Times Books.

Spence, D. (1984). *Narrative Truth and Historical Truth: Meaning and Interpretation in Psychoanalysis*. New York: W. W. Norton.

Spurling, L. (2015). *The Psychoanalytic Craft*. London: Palgrave.

Steiner, J. (1985). Turning a blind eye: the cover-up for Oedipus. *International Review of Psychoanalysis, 12*: 161–172.

Steiner, J. (1993). *Psychic Retreats: Pathological Organizations in Psychotic, Neurotic and Borderline Patients*. London and New York: Routledge.

Sterba, R. (1934). The fate of the ego in psychoanalytic therapy. *International Journal of Psycho-Analysis, 15*: 117–126.

Stern, D. (1985). *The Interpersonal World of the Infant*. New York: Basic Books.

Sulloway, F. (1992). Reassessing Freud's case histories. In: T. Gelfand & J. Kerr (Eds.), *Freud and the History of Psychoanalysis*. Hillsdale, NJ: The Analytic Press.

Sweet, A. D., & Miller, I. S. (2016). Bingeing on sobriety: white holes, black holes and time's arrow in the intra-psychic worlds of addicted and substance-abusing patients. *British Journal of Psychotherapy, 32(2)*: 159–174.

Thomas, D. (1957). The force that through the green fuse drives the flower. In: *Collected Poems*. London: Faber.

Tolstoy, L. (1869). *War and Peace*. Trans. A. Briggs. London: Penguin, 2007.

Tuckett, D. (1993). Some thoughts on the presentation and discussion of the clinical material of psychoanalysis. *International Journal of Psycho-Analysis, 74*: 1175–1189.

Turner, J. (2004). A brief history of illusion: Milner, Winnicott, Rycroft. In: J. Pearson (Ed.), *Analyst of the Imagination: The Life and Work of Charles Rycroft*. London: Karnac.

Turp, M. D. (2001). *Psychosomatic Health: The Body and the Word*. London: Palgrave.

Turp, M. D. (2003). *Hidden Self-Harm: Narratives from Psychotherapy*. London: Jessica Kingsley.

Tuttman, S. (1996). Foreword. In: M. Nitsun, *The Anti-Group: Destructive Forces in the Group and Their Creative Potential*. London: Routledge.

Waddell, M. (1989). Experience and identification in George Eliot's novels. *Free Associations, 1*: 72–84.

Watson, P. (2010). *The German Genius: Europe's Third Renaissance, the Second Scientific Revolution and the Twentieth Century*. New York: Simon & Schuster.

Weegmann, M. (2002). Eugene O'Neill's *Hughie* and the grandiose addict. *Psychodynamic Practice, 8(1)*: 21–31.

Weegmann, M. (2007). Group analysis and homosexuality: indifference or hostility? *Group Analysis, 40(1)*: 44–58.

Weegmann, M. (2016). We're all poor nuts and things happen, and we just get mixed in wrong, that's all: lessons for psychotherapy from Eugene O'Neill's *Anna Christie*. *Psychodynamic Practice, 22(2)*: 131–141.

Weegmann, M. (2017). "Over the last sky": Palestine, Palestinians and social memory. In: E. Hopper & H. Weinberg (Eds.), *The Social Unconscious in Persons, Groups and Societies: Mainly Foundation Matrices*, Volume 3. London: Karnac.

Winnicott, D. W. (1958). The capacity to be alone. In: *The Maturational Processes and the Facilitating Environment: Studies in the Theory of Emotional Development*. London: Karnac, 1990.

Winnicott, D. W. (1960). Ego distortions in terms of true and false self. In: *The Maturational Processes and the Facilitating Environment* (pp. 140–152). New York: International Universities Press.

Winnicott, D. W. (1962). Ego integration in child development. In: *The Maturational Processes and the Facilitating Environment* (pp. 56–63). New York: International Universities Press.

Winnicott, D. W. (1966). Creativity and its origins. In: *Playing and Reality* (pp. 76–100). Harmondsworth: Penguin, 1971.

Winnicott, D. W. (1967). The location of cultural experience. In: *Playing and Reality* (pp. 112–121). Harmondsworth: Penguin, 1971.

Winnicott, D. W. (1971a). The place where we live. In: *Playing and Reality* (pp. 122–136). Harmondsworth: Penguin.

Winnicott, D. W. (1971b). *Playing and Reality*. Harmondsworth: Penguin.

Winnicott, D. W. (1974). *Playing and Reality*. London: Penguin.

Wittgenstein, L. (2009). *Philosophical Investigations* (4th edition). London: Wiley-Blackwell.

Yeats, W. B. (1921). "The Second Coming". In: *Michael Robartes and the Dancer*. Dublin: Cuala Press.

Žižek, S. (1992). *Enjoy Your Symptom!* London: Routledge.

Zweig, S. (1943). *The World of Yesterday*. Trans. A. Bell. London: Pushkin Press, 2011.

Index